CASE STUDIES IN

CULTURAL ANTHROPOLOGY

SERIES EDITORS

George and Louise Spindler

STANFORD UNIVERSITY

TOWN AND COUNTRY

IN LOCOROTONDO

Whitewashed facade of a large trullo.

TOWN AND COUNTRY
IN LOCOROTONDO

ANTHONY H. GALT

University of Wisconsin—Green Bay

Harcourt Brace Jovanovich College Publishers

Fort Worth   Philadelphia   San Diego   New York   Orlando   Austin   San Antonio
Toronto   Montreal   London   Sydney   Tokyo

Publisher:	Ted Buchholz
Acquisitions Editor:	Christopher Klein
Project Editor:	Mike Hinshaw
Production Manager:	Erin Gregg
Book Designer:	Brian Salisbury
Cover Design:	Pat Bracken

Library of Congress Cataloging-in-Publication Data

Galt, Anthony H.
    Town and country in Locorotondo / Anthony H. Galt.
        p.   cm. — (Case studies in cultural anthropology)
    Includes bibliographical references.
    ISBN 0-03-073327-8
    1. Ethnology—Italy—Locorotondo.   2. Peasantry—Italy-
-Locorotondo—Case studies.   3. Elite (Social sciences)—Italy-
-Locorotondo—Case studies.   4. Social classes—Italy—Locorotondo-
-History.   5. Locorotondo (Italy)—Social life and customs.
    I. Title.   II. Series.
    GN585.I8G35   1992
    305.5'0945'751—dc20   92-3298
                                                                              CIP

Requests for permission to make copies of any part of the work should be mailed to: Copyrights
and Permissions Department, 8th Floor; Harcourt Brace Jovanovich, Publishers, Orlando, FL
32887.

Address for editorial correspondence:
Harcourt Brace Jovanovich, Publishers; 301 Commerce Street; Suite 3700; Fort Worth, TX 76102

Address for orders:
Harcourt Brace Jovanovich, Publishers; 6277 Sea Harbor Drive; Orlando, FL 32887 1-800-782-
4479, or 1-800-433-0001 (in Florida)

Printed in the United States of America

2 3 4 5 016 9 8 7 6 5 4 3 2 1

Foreword

ABOUT THE SERIES

These case studies in cultural anthropology are designed for students in beginning and intermediate courses in the social sciences, to bring them insights into the richness and complexity of human life as it is lived in different ways, in different places. The authors are men and women who have lived in the societies they write about and who are professionally trained as observers and interpreters of human behavior. Also, the authors are teachers; in their writing, the needs of the student reader remain foremost. It is our belief that when an understanding of ways of life very different from one's own is gained, abstractions and generalizations about the human condition become meaningful.

The scope and character of the series has changed constantly since we published the first case studies in 1960, in keeping with our intention to represent anthropology as it is. We are concerned with the ways in which human groups and communities are coping with the massive changes wrought in their physical and sociopolitical environments in recent decades. We are also concerned with the ways in which established cultures have solved life's problems. And we want to include representation of the various modes of communication and emphasis that are being formed and reformed as anthropology itself changes.

We think of this series as an instructional series, intended for use in the classroom. We, the editors, have always used case studies in our teaching, whether for beginning students or advanced graduate students. We start with case studies, whether from our own series or from elsehwere, and weave our way into theory, and then turn again to cases. For us, they are the grounding of our discipline.

ABOUT THE AUTHOR

Anthony H. Galt was born in Hollywood, California in 1944. He studied anthropology as an undergraduate during the tumultous 1960s at the University of California at Berkeley, missing the famous Free Speech Movement only because he spent 1964–65 immersing himself in Northern Italian university life and the Italian language in the University of California's Education Abroad Program at the venerable University of Padua in Italy. Although, hardly a campus activist during those years, the movements of the time inspired him to think about how societies change and what social change means to people. He chose to study Italian and to go to Padua because of a love for the sound of language, and because his mother provided him with an Italian American heritage about which he was curious. Having achieved Italian fluency at Padua, he finished an anthropology major at Berkeley and decided to pursue his Ph.D. in Anthropology at the University of California at

Riverside. With a dissertation about a village on the Italian island, Pantelleria, he obtained his doctoral degree in 1971.

Since then he has taught courses in antrhopology, social science theory and methods, and changing American rural society, in an unusual interdisciplinary academic setting called the Concentration in Social Change and Development at the University of Wisconsin—Green Bay. This institution was founded in the late 1960s as an experimental campus that would reorganize teaching and research along interdisciplinary lines. This meant that Galt came into regular contact with colleagues who were economists, political scientists, historians, psychologists, and sociologists, as well as anthropologists. Such contact, in a department devoted to the interdisciplinary study of social change, influenced his approach. In the 1970s he began producing a series of articles about various aspects of life on Pantelleria and then in 1981–82 completed fieldwork and archival research in Italy about Locorotondo, the subject of this book. His main interests have included magic, political relationships, the ecology and economy of agricultural activities, marriage fertility, social stratification, and social change as experienced by working people and elites in the South of Italy. Interests in social change, and daily contact with colleagues doing history and writing about the nature of history, strongly influenced the historical approach seen in this book and in other recent writings. His next project is to apply some anthropological conceptual tools to an analysis of early nineteenth century revolutionary secret societies in Southern Italy, such as the Carboneria. To that end he spent the summer of 1989 leafing through historical documents in many provincial archives in Southern Italy.

ABOUT THIS CASE STUDY

Town and Country in Locorotondo is the latest addition to a collection of case studies on European cultural groups that began in 1962 with the publication of *Vasilika: A Village in Modern Greece* by Ernestine Friedl. This title is still in print, but with the exception of Jeremy Bossevain's *Village in Malta,* none of the 13 case studies on European places and people published between that date and 1980 have survived in this series. In 1990 we published Sue Parman's *Scottish Crofters: A Historical Ethnography of a Celtic Village.* This excellent study seems to be meeting with the approval of our colleagues. And *Nazare: Women and Men in a Prebureaucratic Portugese Fishing Village* will have appeared by the time *Locorotondo* is published.

As editors of an instructional series intended for use in undergraduate courses, we wanted to move from the heavy emphasis on exotic (as seen by western eyes) cultures to those closer to home and an obvious part of the complex, literate, modern world. It isn't that we thought of the "exotic" cultures as unimportant—we use them for a basic part of our teaching in introductory anthropology—but we felt the relevance of anthropology to the modern scene needed to be demonstrated, especially for students who were most likely taking their first, and last, anthropology course. To this end we published the European studies and a group of American cases as well. The publisher was willing to experiment, and we can thank their open-minded editors and managers for the opportunity to do so (particularly, of course, David Boynton, who was always interested in something new). However, they were not willing to hold case studies in print, at considerable expense, that were used much less widely than were the more "exotic" titles. It was clear that the anthropological market was not ready for case studies on contemporary European and American cultural groups, despite the interest expressed in such studies and the considerable activity of anthropologists in these fields. Since the case studies are used mainly in introductory and intermediate level courses, we conclude that the instructors of these courses were not including Europe and the United States in their presentations or requirements. It may be that the most conservative attributes of anthropology show most clearly in the introductory courses and that the image of the anthropologist as the hardy, resourceful explorer enduring hardships in remote jungles and deserts, or on a remote Pacific island, was more intriguing (so the instructors might think) to undergraduates, than the image of the anthropologist as a student of a European or State-side community, living in an apartment or house, however rude, and buying food at the local grocery store or supermarket.

Perhaps the emphasis on the "exotic" and remote in anthropology is inevitable, and has served us well as a distinguishing criterion. Otherwise, how are we to be seen as different than sociologists, or other social scientists who do field work? We are getting better at explaining ourselves, and indeed, the pervasive influence of anthropological preoccupations upon the faculty in literature, philosophy, education, law, medicine, etc., suggests whatever it is we have done or do, it is interesting and somehow relevant to non-anthropologists as well as our colleagues in anthropology. The cultures of the most distinctive "others" may be our most important subject matter, since it is these ways of life, as interpreted by anthropologists, that most dramatically challenge our assumptions, values, and world views, and rock the ethnocentrism of our students' work decisively.

However, the sudden growth of the Society for the Anthropology of Europe, the number of articles published in our professional journals on European culture groups and communities, the emergence of some positions for "Europeanist" anthropologists, and particularly the growing number of papers given and panels held at the national and regional meetings of our discipline, suggest there is growing interest in European studies. Though not a movement, there is a development that augers well for another try at case studies representing the work of anthropologists in Europe.

Locorotondo is a worthy contribution to this attempt. It is foreign, at times exotic, to our American eyes. It is familiar enough to seem almost comfortable, but strange enough to be interesting. Anthony Galt, himself of Italian extraction on the maternal side, does well in his development of both the strange and the familiar. Both can be seen in intimate detail, based upon a close, virtually "native-like" relationship with the people and their community. His long, indepth field work and his several returns to the research site over the years have made possible this intimate relationship between ethnographic observations and people, and his own ethnic heritage has certainly helped.

The author's approach to Locorotondo and its environs is both contemporary and historical. He moves easily between the past and the present and keeps an eye cocked toward change in all the institutions and relationships he pursues. He avoids a common entrapment—an exclusive focus on peasant lives and culture—and places peasants as well as artisans, elites, bureaucrats and bureaucracy in the larger context of relationships and perceptions.

He gives his informants voices, which they use to good effect in conversations recorded and reproduced on the pages of this case study. There is a modernist, perhaps postmodernist touch to much of what he writes, and yet the grounding of interpretation in observation and recorded behavior is never neglected. And he puts himself, and occasionally his family, into the picture. He concludes this study with a chapter on Locorotondo in southern Italian perspective, attending to how the Locorotondesi distinguish themselves from other peoples, how they see themselves within their region, and how Locorotondo may be distinguised from other places. Having experienced this chapter in this case study, one misses something like it in many other studies.

Town and Country in Locorotondo has much to teach undergraduate readers about an Italian place and about anthropology. We will use it in Antrhopology 001 for both reasons. It will also be of interest to professionals and advance students, as a significant addition to the existing Euro-ethnographic literature.

George and Louise Spindler
Series Editors
Ethnographics, P. O. Box 38
Calistoga, CA 94515

ACKNOWLEDGMENTS

I could not have researched and written this book without the help of many people and several institutions. I carried out the original research in the field during the academic year 1981–82 with a grant from the National Science Foundation. My university, the University of Wisconsin—Green Bay, also supplied some funding and released time for the analysis of data, as well as partial support for a return visit during the summer of 1986. In Locorotondo, many interviewees and friends facilitated my ethnographic and oral historical studies. I did most interviewing with the promise of anonymity so I cannot thank them personally, and I have changed the names of the interviewees whose words I reproduce here. Above all, however, let me thank Giorgio Cardone, my friend and colleague at arms in Locorotondo who helped with the difficulties of local dialect, lined up interviews, explained many things, and bounced ideas back and forth with me for many an hour. Others in Locorotondo who deserve my thanks are Michele Gianfrate, then mayor, who facilitated our settling in, Franco Basile, who contributed many insights, and our friends Dino and Livia Crovace. Livia, in particular, went far beyond my expectations, when, in response to some queries about artisan courtship and marriage that I made to her in a letter, she did a series of taped interviews with friends and relatives. I have incorporated some of the things she collected in chapter 5.

I want to thank Don Dean, Holt, Rinehart and Winston representative, for suggesting that I write this book. Those who participated in the review process at Holt, Rinehart and Winston, then, later, Harcourt Brace Jovanovich, including especially the Anthropology editor Chris Klein, and the series editors, George and Louise Spindler, as well as the reviewers, helped me shape a more attractive book. As always my colleagues in Social Change and Development at the University of Wisconsin—Green Bay, lent moral support. Finally, my wife, Janice, and my son Alex, enjoyed the fieldwork, both of them growing from it, as I did. They then encouraged me through the years of data analysis and writing up that produced this work and several others. Janice read and commented upon the next to final draft of this manuscript.

Anthony H. Galt
Green Bay, Wisconsin

Contents

Illustrations

CHAPTER EIGHT

To my father,

Wendell W. Galt

1 / Introduction

Suppose that we meet at the railroad station in Bari. To reach Locorotondo we leave the urban tangle of that seaside regional capital, happily freeing ourselves of its one-way streets and "macho" driving, and proceed southeast on the super highway through the coastal plain of central Apulia past the ports of Mola, Polignano a Mare, and Monopoli, toward Fasano. To either side of the freeway stretches a sea of olive trees—each pruned into a gray-green cube. To the left there is an occasional glimpse of the Adriatic Sea; to the right beyond the groves rise highlands known locally as the Plateau of the Trulli.

Just before the outskirts of Fasano a road marked "Taranto" diverges and leads up to the plateau and over it to the gulf that forms Italy's instep. The road climbs past the turn-off to Zoosafari, a wild animal park built for tourists seeking a change from beach lolling on the nearby Fasanese coast during their August holidays. The road is narrow and hangs on the side of the steep cliffs that jut upwards to form the northern edge of the Plateau of the Trulli. We pass a lone bicycle racer, off the

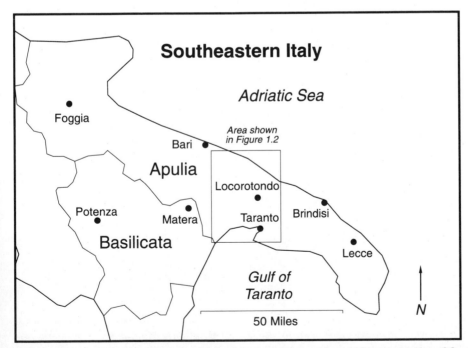

Figure 1.1 Map of southeastern Italy showing the location of Locorotondo with repsect to large cities.

saddle, standing on his pedals as he trains his muscles on the steep climb. Local drivers worry about finding the Highway Police waiting along this road to pull over vehicles they suspect have equipment violations. Fines can be large and payable on the spot and somehow the police manage to find something wrong with each vehicle they stop. Those whose autos will not pass inspection, or truck drivers carrying loads without proper papers, take an ancient engine-straining back road that runs steeply and directly up a ravine from Fasano to the plateau's edge.

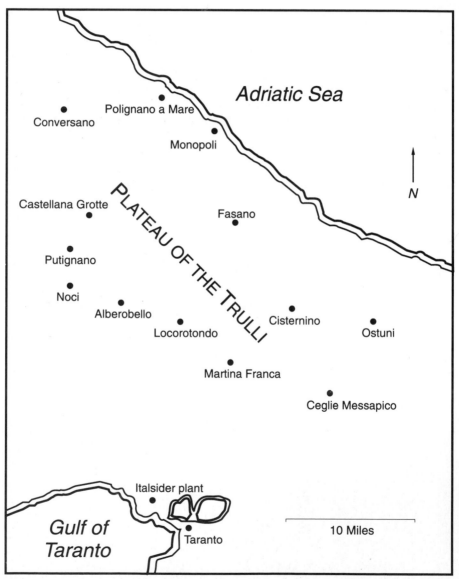

Figure 1.2   Map of the Plateau of the Trulli zone showing major towns mentioned in the text.

We climb still more and crest at Laureto, a cluster of buildings—a bar, a pizzeria, a roadside fruit stand, and a scattering of small villas. People from below annually capture the northern edge of the plateau to escape the oppressive heat of the Fasano lowlands. They move up into the cooler climate, leaving behind those without the means to own or rent a summer place.

Now we quickly cross into the territory of Locorotondo, this book's focus. We also realize why the zone is called the Plateau of the Trulli, for to all sides, dotted here and there among lush vineyards, small orchards, and grain fields, are the roof cones of local peasant dwellings called *trulli* in Italian. A trullo is a complex of thick-walled rooms, each capped by a cone built by cantilevering successively smaller circles of stone over one another until they close at the top, and covered on the outside with limestone slabs arranged in overlapping circles like shingles. Decorative knobs top each cupola. These pinnacles and the walls of each building are freshly whitewashed each year and shine brightly in the sun in strong contrast with the dark slate gray of the weathered roof cones.

The nearby town of Alberobello, which contains whole neighborhoods of trulli, is a destination for tourists seeking exotic sights. But trulli are anything but exotic to those who live in them. In fact, as we proceed along the road we notice that the landscape also contains many recently built cement block houses, more spaciously constructed without roof cones. The tourists probably wish for the view of fifty years ago in which only the gray-coned country dwellings would have met their eyes. Tourists, who often travel to escape the humdrum reality of their own lives,

Figure 1.3   Isolated trullo beyond an olive grove.

find it difficult to accept the reality of the lives of those who live in the place of escape.

The road leads on. An old man driving a motorscooter with a cab hauling a miniature truck bed with a rototiller in it hugs the right side of the road as his tiny engine grinds up the hill. We pass cautiously. To the right in the distance, beyond an expanse of vineyards, appears the hill community of San Marco, the largest rural settlement in the municipality of Locorotondo. The hill is crowned with a large trullo-domed church—a symbol of the community identity of the San Marco dwellers. Side roads join the national highway from either side inviting us to explore the country landscape, but we feel compelled by the speed of the traffic to drive on along this narrow but heavily traveled route toward the town. Trees planted just at the edge of the paving stimulate thoughts of tragic impact. To the left we pass a large furniture store isolated in the countryside. To the right sits a rose colored trullo tobacco shop. Behind it in a vineyard a man turns his rototiller to churn the soil between another row of grape vines. Cement block buildings become more common. To the right appears a quarry, and then off the road a small factory that makes wallpaper-sample–binders from vinyl and markets them internationally.

Now, crowning a high ridge on the horizon, loom Locorotondo's bell towers and domes, partially obscured by new condominiums. This view of Locorotondo from the countryside has local symbolic meanings. Those meanings crystallize in a dialect proverb that goes: *Ce ui mangé u pen, stè lunten dé campen.*[1] "If you want to eat bread, stay away from the church bells." The bells are in the tall spire of the church of Saint George, visible, when hills do not intervene, from the farthest edges of the town's rural territory. It is a peasant proverb that expresses the experiences of the urban and rural cultures of Locorotondo and, to a lesser extent, the surrounding towns. Here is a zone in Southern Italy where peasants have not been dirt poor, but

Figure 1.4   Bell towers and condominiums in Locorotondo seen across a country landscape including a trullo hamlet.

have managed to capture land, live in the countryside semi-independently from large landowners, and wrest a living growing their own food and raising grapes for market. The proverb implies that a working man—an artisan—who lives in town is worse off.

Speeding on, to the left we see another concrete building, and a small garment factory, then a gas station and the edge of town—hardly the most picturesque entrance to Locorotondo. This side of town is the expanding edge, and it is a jumble of recently built apartment houses and post-World War II public housing. There is an auto dealer, a mechanic or two, a restaurant, and another gas station. It is a townscape we could find anywhere in Italy in a sprawling town or city margin. I have chosen to lead you into town by this route because it reflects present reality in Locorotondo better than other more picturesque ways. From another direction the astonishing view of the curved white edge of town formed by the pitch-roofed houses of the historic center is only tenuously preserved from obliteration by the abrupt slope below—almost a cliff—that is too steep for construction of reinforced concrete condominiums.

The road takes us into Piazza Marconi, the automobile hub of Locorotondo, from which six routes radiate to other destinations. It is late morning. The town bustles with activity. Those wishing to continue to Martina Franca or beyond to Taranto, must challenge the chaotic traffic that converges here. From Piazza Marconi the major artery of the town slants upward to the left and leads us on an architectural journey: It travels from the twentieth-century surroundings of the traffic glut, past nineteenth-century stores and houses, past Piazza Aldo Moro and the blocky post-Fascist municipal hall, past appliance and clothing stores and coffee bars, to crest between the mid-nineteenth-century gate to the historical center to the left, and the cool green municipal gardens to the right. Everywhere sidewalks and benches, doorsteps and walls, host men, old and young, talking and gesturing, or just watching the social scene, as many women shop, plastic bags of groceries dangling from their hands. To penetrate the historical center of Locorotondo we must alight from the car.

We pass between two monumental square pillars and step into a space, known simply as the *piazza* (the square) because once it was the only one. It is no longer the commercial or administrative center of Locorotondo, and even at peak hours, such as during this business day morning or the afternoon social promenade, we find it relatively quiet, its steps occupied only by a few lounging shopkeepers waiting for customers and chatting with passers-by. There is Orazio, the friendly cobbler turned shoe salesman, and Martino, the excellent barber whose shop is encrusted with swirling "liberty style" ornaments calculated to appeal to the gentlemen of the turn of the century.

When I first went with my family to Locorotondo in 1981, I needed a haircut. (In fact I had avoided having one before the trip because I knew from previous ethnographic work that barbers can be good initial contacts in Italian towns—they know many people and their business.) I found Martino's shop on our third afternoon in Locorotondo. While he artfully cut my hair, I shared with him my reasons for coming to the town and asked about a house. He said that he would ask around. We began to talk about the town and the countryside, and he noted that his business would pick up around 7:00 P.M. when peasant men would come into town

Figure 1.5   The monumental pillars that frame the entrance to the historical center of Locorotondo.

to make a few evening purchases, and get a hair cut or a shave. He spoke with admiration for their prosperity and industriousness and boasted to me that as a measure of local prosperity the ratio of cars to people in Locorotondo was second only to Milan. His admiration for the local peasantry, it turned out, was not necessarily shared by others belonging to the town's artisan group, and the boast about car registration appears to be a myth trucked out for strangers to emphasize local prosperity that can be found in other towns (I had already heard it elsewhere), but I knew from my travels and readings that his observations did reflect unusual realities for the *mezzogiorno*—the Italian south.

From the piazza and Martino's shop we follow narrow streets in a labyrinth, penetrable only by the smallest of automobiles, that guarantees loss of way for both unfamiliar visitors and local country dwellers. Those whose doors open onto the streets and alleys keep the foot-polished stone paving scrupulously free of litter and rubbish. The walls of houses two and three stories high, kept clean and bright as desert-bleached bones by summer whitewashing, surround us. Occasional inscriptions over windows and doorways date the houses—each the result of numerous remodelings and modifications—to the nineteenth, eighteenth, seventeenth, and sometimes sixteenth centuries. Here and there is a portal bearing on its keystone a coat of arms testifying to past demonstrations of, or pretensions to, nobility, power,

Figure 1.6 Narrow street in Locorotondo's historical center. Note the pitch-roofed town house.

and wealth. But our senses are soon distracted from architectural matters by the odors of midday cooking: garlic or onion frying golden in savory local olive oil to start a sauce for a heaping plate of pasta.

Most ground floor doorways open into single-room apartments. A few of them still contain a lone old tailor who will tell of the days in which tailors' shops teemed with apprentices, and how difficult it is now to earn an artisan's living because of industrial competition. They tell how Locorotondo was a town full of tailors—an exporter of tailors—and that tailors were the kings of the artisan world; and how, even so, they made a poor living in the old days because they could charge so little, there being so many of them. Often they had only pasta to eat.

By following the meanderings of the widest street, we come to a narrow open square dominated on one side by a large tan church with a statue of Saint George and his dragon enemy centered in the triangular pediment over the entrance. Saint George is one of Locorotondo's patrons and protectors. This is the parish church, the seat of the Archpriest, the starting point of most processions, and the final wayside in a procession to the cemetery for most Locorotondesi—artisan, peasant, merchant, professional, or old landowner, alike.

The bells of San Giorgio, already spotted from the countryside, and of the smaller church, San Rocco, inspire the peasants' proverbial warning to avoid town. Compared to the peasants' life in the open, the enclosed life of the artisans, clustered around the churches in one-room dwellings, was often poor and typified by hunger. The artisan's image of the peasant house is one jammed with cheeses, great jars of wine, crocks of olive oil, sacks of grain and fava beans, and mounds of dried figs. Old artisans envied peasants, but also put them down as less than civilized. Some townspeople still hold such attitudes. Once, while I made a deposit at the bank, a teller who was the son of a local artisan family asked me why I had come to Locorotondo to live. I answered that I had come to study *"civiltà contadina,"* then a catch phrase in Italian academic and intellectual circles that literally translates as "peasant civilization," but more properly means "peasant culture." He smiled at my response and volunteered that "peasants have no *civiltà.*"

Things have changed, but the time when Locorotondo contained two clearly separated cultures is well remembered by middle-aged adults. Then, as is still much the case, all peasants lived outside the town in the countryside and almost all artisans—the tailors, the shoemakers, the carpenters, the blacksmiths, the saddlemakers, the barrelmakers, the barbers, the masons—lived cheek by jowl in the town, sharing the squares with professionals, merchants, a few landowning gentlemen, and two social outcast groups, carters and herders. Now the countryside is occupied by aging agriculturalists and their sons and daughters, many of whom have turned into craftsmen and contractors in lucrative construction trades. But, there are still strong differences in world view between town and country people.

This division was, and still is, unusual for South Italy. In most southern towns only a tiny proportion of the population lives in the countryside, and peasants are often just as urban as other working class members of the population. I remember my surprise once in Western Sicily when a friend, who graciously took my wife and me on a drive, pointed to what we thought was a large city crowning a hill across a valley from where we had parked, called it a "village," and noted that it was inhabited mostly by peasant workers. The "agrotown" is the rule in Southern Italy. Instead, Locorotondo has, and long has had, the highest percentage of rural resident population in the area. Now just over half of Locorotondo's people live outside the confines of the town. The figure has been as high as two-thirds.

Continuing our stroll, we take a few turns through narrow alleys and join a slightly wider artery that leads past the Cooperative Bookstore, an enterprise begun by several unemployed leftist college students. Here there is always a conversation. Descending now we spot Locorotondo's second most important church, San Rocco. Saint Rocco is the town's other patron, and his festival held in the middle of August musters emigrants from elsewhere in Italy and Europe to visit their relatives and reestablish their identities with Locorotondo. The streets fill with cars bearing foreign and out of region plates. We turn left in front of San Rocco and soon encounter an opening with a downward stairway. From this vantage point we see a piece of the countryside stretching before us. There are hills and valleys visible, and a road leading off into the distance. Everywhere there are houses, many of them trulli. It is a crowded, lushly cultivated countryside. If we stood in a similar spot in many other Southern Italian towns what we would see would be quite different. We would look out on an empty countryside, with perhaps some vineyards, gardens, and orchards in the immediate foreground and vast expanses of wheat fields beyond. In some areas, parts of Basilicata[2] for example, it would be hard to distinguish any rural settlement, or even any crops growing—only barren eroded hills, badlands.

This has been a hypothetical trip into Locorotondo. Most readers probably will never go there even if they go to Italy; few American visitors get beyond the three big meccas: Florence, Venice, and Rome. It is, however, far easier to take than the trips many anthropological colleagues make into deserts, across mountains, through tropical forests, or into arctic tundras to reach the people they study. In fact, given the means and a little luck, we could probably arrive in Locorotondo tomorrow— it is a flight to Rome and a rental car away. If it is easily reached, if it is not so exotic as, say, an Amazonian Indian village, why is it the stuff of anthropological study? What is compelling and interesting about it as a place? How can we ask anthropological questions about it that illuminate our understanding of humanity?

Locorotondo is a European place. The serious study of European locales is only a recent development in cultural anthropology. The first studies appeared in the 1930s, but it was not until the 1950s that a steady trickle of work began. The 1980s have seen a much greater degree of interest in the area. But, because of its orientation—some would say bias—toward more exotic and non-western societies, cultural anthropology has not embraced the idea of studying European populations wholeheartedly. There are still major graduate departments, for instance, with specialists in most of the rest of the world, but with no anthropologist specializing in Europe.[3]

Beyond the basic idea that anthropologists ought to take all of humanity into their scope, why are European places good field sites for anthropologists? They are part of complex societies and have been for millennia. Each village, each town, each city, contains a variety of people divided by things such as ethnicity (Gypsies and locals, for instance), social class, and occupation. In turn each village and each town an anthropologist might visit has administrative, economic, and social relationships with other places, some at a parallel level in terms of size and power, and others at higher levels. Such relationships imply bureaucracies at each level. Because of this they are places with astonishingly detailed historical records. It often takes a high degree of detective work to tease out of the archives the kinds of historical records that tell us about ordinary people, but it is possible.

These facts make European settings ideal for looking at questions about social change and about the relationship of local places to the larger entities that engulf them—regions, states, and spheres of trade. For instance, several books published by anthropologists and fellow travelers about Sicily set a pattern for subsequent scholars interested in Italy to incorporate historical research and analysis in their work (Schneider and Schneider, 1976; Blok, 1974). It no longer seems sufficient merely to describe social organization, for instance; it has become equally important to look at its historical emergence and how it changes. If we observe institutions as ethnographic fieldworkers, how far back in time do they go, how do they emerge, how do they change through time? How do local processes of change relate to greater patterns of change such as the formation of national states, the end of feudalism, and the rise of socially and economically liberal regimes? In the twentieth century how do local processes relate to events like world wars, the rise and fall of fascism and communism, and in Western Europe the greater democratization of society, and the on-going process of European unification? The historically rich European setting often makes answers to these kinds of questions possible for the anthropologist interested in the lives of everyday people. In this short monograph I will not pretend to explore all these important questions for Locorotondo, but the approach informs my analysis and motivates the decision to include the next chapter, "Locorotondo in Time," and the historical descriptions that will follow in later chapters.[4]

What kinds of questions does an encounter with Locorotondo stir up? I have implied some of them in the tour that begins this chapter, an excursion like my first visit to the place, and similar to brief tours I've given visiting friends and relatives. The first question is, simply put: why is this place special among Southern Italian places, and what are the implications of its being special? Its rural architecture is special (and it has been amply described elsewhere), but I fear we will never find a totally satisfying answer about how it developed. What is also special, however, is the fact that it (along with some neighboring places) is an "oasis of small property in an area of large estates," as a turn of the century Italian geographer colorfully wrote. It is also peculiar because here peasants actually moved outside the town walls during the late eighteenth and early nineteenth centuries to produce the sharp contrast between town and country. That contrast demands exploration, and will be a major theme in the next chapter and in the final chapter of this monograph.

A second theme I will stress is that of social change. How and why has Locorotondo changed from a state that its current inhabitants think of as traditional to a state in which local issues and usages, and the lives of local people, are more greatly integrated with things emanating from central places—Rome and Bari among others? Here a major concern is deciding what remains unique and special about Locorotondo and what is conditioned and created by its relationship with larger spheres like the market for wine and the Italian political system.

It is also important to consider how change has conditioned the experiences of individuals from various parts of Locorotondese society. A useful way for thinking about this derives from C. Wright Mills' goal of the "sociological imagination" (1959, Chapter 1, in particular). Mills taught that useful social science always pays attention to the kinds of people produced in particular historical eras and social organizations, in short, to the connection between change, society, and biography. Further, for particular populations he instructed us to explore "what values are cherished yet threatened, and what values are cherished and supported, by the characterizing trends of [a] period. In the case of both threat and support we must ask what salient contradictions of structure may be involved." For Locorotondo we need to understand how the values men and women grew up with in an era they now see as gone—for some purposes as "the good old days," and for others as "the bad old days,"—have become threatened and compromised. If we can look at such predicaments in Locorotondo and in other places, perhaps with the curious stereoscopic vision anthropology offers us, we can reflect better upon change, structure, and biography in our own society. To do this I am going to stress the idea of career, both narrowly in the sense of jobs, and more broadly in the sense of experiences, such as marriage, everyday people have had during their lives. When I arrived most adult Locorotondese had begun with different expectations of how their lives would go than they actually turned out. Social and economic change had strongly intervened in the decades after World War II such that the expectations people grew up with became, in many cases, impossible to realize.

With reference to these ideas I want to consider the theme of politics and political power in Locorotondo. No discussion of institutions or change in Italy can be adequate without considering politics and political parties, so pervasive are their direct and indirect affects on everyday events in peoples' lives; Locorotondo is no different. I will portray a small town's Southern Italian politics as it pervades the lives of its citizens through the relationship of what I call the official system and the real system. I will show how men and women obtain power for themselves and their parties through what are called patron client relationships, in which rules are selectively bent by those with power for those who are without it in exchange for the future loyalty or help of the latter.

The concept of culture I have adopted, then, emphasizes expectations people come to have and the strategies they develop to lead their lives satisfactorily. Culture must not be seen as a rigid structure. At best, it is a set of ideas about how things work that people pick up throughout their lives. In a complex society such as that of Locorotondo, some of it comes from childhood experiences, some of it from schooling, some of it from belonging to a generation and undergoing its experiences, some of it from sources like television and radio, and some of it from the process of maturing in a changing society. Culture provides people with expectations about their chances in life and it informs their strategic decisions about how to lead a life in a given society.

I will therefore also bring to my observations about Locorotondo what I consider an important model for the understanding of social change as it relates to social groupings and to the individuals within them, particularly in a situation of social complexity such as a modern Southern European town. This is the idea of adaptive strategy, a concept that was elaborated by a cultural anthropologist named John Bennett, and that is useful because it helps us think about how individuals and populations develop conscious, but often not perfect or even totally successful, plans for dealing with the limits and opportunities in their natural and social environments. (See Bennett, 1969, for a longer discussion.) In a complex social situation such as that of Locorotondo we can use the concept to consider how people in definable subgroups formulate strategies to cope with external change and with the interests and strategies of other local subgroups.

Some models of adaptiveness assume that whatever institutions exist in a society are there because they have been adaptive, or functional—because they have facilitated the continuity of society, or ensured its survival. Such ideas were typical of a theoretical school in anthropology called "functionalism." They were also commonly found in the anthropological subdiscipline known as "cultural ecology." Bennett's notion of adaptive strategy need not be applied in this way, because it allows that strategies that groups formulate do not always work, or that they may only work in the short run. It may even be that the strategy of one group may be foiled by the strategy of another in situations of conflict and contradiction. The idea invites us to think about the interests of various groups in a complex society and because strategies emerge in response to change, it invites us to think in historical terms about processes. I find the concept congenial for thinking about the groups and individuals I have learned about in Locorotondo, both in the present from talking with people, and in the past through historical detective work.

Here then is a book about a special place in the south of Italy. It is a place with much to recommend it for study, both scientifically and aesthetically. I chose it because of rational scientific reasons: it seemed a distillation of the characteristics of the region where it is located as measured by censuses, and it is of a size (11,000 people divided about equally between town and countryside) that seemed at the time possible to study. But I also chose it because its beauty immediately struck me. My family and I wanted to live there for a year instead of in a neighboring town like tourist-ridden Alberobello, or larger, more bustling and complex Martina Franca.

We settled there for the academic year 1981-1982 in a hamlet named Lamie d'Olimpia. My son Alex began his grade school career in a rural school with six local children and my wife Janice and I began the process of adapting again to country life. My studies were a combination of historical documents research aimed at discovering the causes and consequences of the area's unusual settlement pattern over the long term, and of ethnographic research aimed at understanding the town in the present and recent past.

I base this book on interviews and experiences during that year, and upon our experiences there during the summer of 1986 when we again lived for two months in Lamie among old friends while I commuted daily to Bari to continue my historical studies. I found that, unlike my previous ethnographic work on the island of Pantelleria near Sicily, because Locorotondo was so large I could not rely merely upon participant observation in the hamlet in which we settled. Instead, I had to conduct formal interviews all over the territory and town with as many kinds of people—peasants, agricultural workers, construction worker/part-time peasants, craftsmen, merchants, professionals, and old landowners—as I could. My place of residence and the nature of my project led me to stress rural Locorotondo over the town scene, however. I constructed guidelines for most of these open-ended interviews with an eye toward understanding social change as it had affected the lives of the people I talked to. This work was greatly enriched by the presence of my friend and colleague Giorgio Cardone who helped with dialect problems and lent his intuitions—gleaned from having grown up in a rural family, but having also completed a university degree and found a niche in the local educational system then as a middle school teacher—to the formulation of our interviews. In addition, and again with Giorgio Cardone's indispensable help, I carried out a sample survey of households in the countryside to collect basic socioeconomic data.

Before describing Locorotondo's present, it is important to understand something of its history. The town has seen rapid social change over the last several decades, but this does not mean that things stood still before then. What local people perceive to be traditional times—as the baseline of change within their individual experiences—were themselves the result of highly significant changes on the local level in the past several centuries. To understand the present of a place like Locorotondo one must also understand certain important facts about its past.

NOTES

1. This is an example of the dialect spoken in Locorotondo—a member of the central Apulian dialects of Italian and mutually unintelligible with the national language. I have adopted an orthography based upon standard Italian spellings. The character "e," however, is pronounced as in French "de" when it appears without an accent, and with an accent (é, è) also more or less as in French. The unaccented "e" often combines with other vowels to produce diphthongs that are characteristic of local speech.

2. The zone constituting the instep of the Italian boot, dry and barren, except in the high mountains.

3. Also, throughout his recent book, *Anthropology Through the Looking Glass* (1987), Michael Herzfeld convincingly argues that the anthropology of modern European communities has not caught the discipline's attention because it is discomforting. Throughout the history of the discipline, he asserts that anthropologists have often been important as definers of "the exotic other." Uncomfortable contradictions are created when ethnographers train their sights on European communities because they are too close to home.

4. I have also explored some of these questions in my more professionally-oriented book on the town, *Far from the Church Bells: Settlement and Society in an Apulian Town*, which is largely a historical analysis of the unusual settlement pattern of Locorotondo and the social and political consequences that have emerged with it (Galt, 1991a).

2 / Locorotondo in Time

No one knows exactly when Locorotondo first became a settlement. A local amateur archaeologist has found stone tools and other artifacts that suggest the site has been used by humans since the upper paleolithic, as far back as perhaps 20,000 years ago, but no systematic archaeology has ever been done in the area. Its location on a route—no more than a trail in antiquity—that led from the Adriatic coast up and over the heel of Italy toward the ancient city of Taranto may have promoted continuous settlement on and near the ridge the current town occupies. However great its antiquity, the settlement at the ridge was never very large, and until the later middle ages probably formed no more than a collection of shepherds' huts in a vast, heavily wooded zone.

The settlement grew just inland from the edge of a large plateau from which one looks down upon the coastal strip bordered by the Adriatic Sea. Locorotondo first appears in written history in 1086 A.D. as the Hamlet of Saint George (still its patron saint), part of a feudal grant to the Abbey of Saint Stephen in Fasano (Sampietro, 1922: 42). The name Locorotondo first crops up in 1276 (Baccaro, 1968: 64-65). No building currently standing in the town dates back farther than the fifteenth century when, according to a Spanish tax register, the settlement numbered sixty-five hearths, or between two and three hundred people (Guarella, 1983: 76). The walls and towers that enclosed the town until the middle of the last century dated from the late fifteenth century and may have been a response to threats of marauding Turks (Baccaro, 1968: 80). During the early fifteenth century the town passed from religious feudal jurisdiction (under The Knights of Malta) into the hands of secular lords. It continued to pass back and forth between them as a small token in the serious games of wealth and inheritance noble men and women played. Ultimately, in 1645 it became a barony of the Caracciolo family, a powerful noble lineage in the Kingdom of Naples, and the Dukes of neighboring Martina Franca (Baccaro, 1968: 89).

The Italian word that designates the area making up a town (or city) center and its rural hinterlands is *commune*, which can best be translated as "municipality." The rural territory that forms the municipality of Locorotondo began to take shape in 1566 when the Crown assigned to towns rights of administration over land within a vast stretch of surrounding woodlands. The amounts were determined according to the town's population numbers. The aim was to end illegal walling off of fields on common land that was supposed to be open for local residents (Sampietro, 1922: 254-263).

Locorotondo remained under feudal jurisdiction of the Dukes of Martina Franca, also the Barons of Locorotondo, until the abolition of feudalism in 1806. This meant

Figure 2.1   The late sixteenth century Palace of the Dukes of Martina Franca (and Barons of Locorotondo) in Martina Franca.

that the enforcement of law and order in its territory lay mostly in the hands of magistrates appointed by its feudal lord. The individual who held the noble title at a given moment could be very arbitrary in his use of authority. During the early eighteenth century, for instance, being sent by the Duke into confinement in Locorotondo was a fearsome thing because it meant imprisonment in a large hole excavated under the castle into which prisoners were lowered on a rope and left to rot (Cofano, 1977: 143). Feudalism also meant that the lord could exact fees and tributes from the population living within his jurisdiction, although throughout the second half of the eighteenth century a rising landowning middle class succeeded in depriving him of these rights by advancing complex legal arguments about the original land concession in 1566 in front of a royal court (Baccaro, 1968: 90).

Feudalism usually meant that a large amount of territory in a municipality was set aside as common land to which all local inhabitants could have access for activities such as hunting, gathering firewood and wild plants, and pasturing. Eighteenth-century records refer to various kinds of common lands, but also suggest that they had earlier fallen into private ownership. Unfortunately, no records survive that show how this happened, but by the middle of that century there was a considerable amount of land in the hands of small proprietor peasants. Patterns that would typify Locorotondo in the future were already underway.

French occupation in 1805, a result of Napoleon's conquest of the Italian boot, led to the abrupt abolition of feudalism in the Kingdom of Naples a year later. The Duke of Martina Franca retained full ownership of two large estates—mostly in woods—but soon sold them, ending his direct influence on the town.[1] During the late eighteenth century and especially during the early nineteenth, a set of families of middle class origins grew rich and dominant, but not without struggle among them. In 1816, that struggle lead to the grisly murder of the son of a powerful family by members of the opposing faction who hired the services of a notorious bandit. These families, and a handful of others, would remain the richest and most powerful in the town until after the Fascist era more than a century later. Some of them acquired pieces of the ex-ducal estates.

While this landowning middle class grew powerful, more peasants acquired land and moved from within the town walls out into the countryside to complete the settlement pattern described in the opening chapter. This process occurred in waves, beginning perhaps in the early eighteenth century and continuing into the late nineteenth. It can be followed statistically only at certain dates from certain kinds of records. A census taken in 1811 shows, for instance, that a little over one third of Locorotondo's population lived outside the walls.[2] By the second Italian government census, taken in 1871, fully two thirds of the population lived rurally (Liuzzi, 1981: 99). The movement of peasants outside the walls threatened local gentlemen, probably because it deprived them of town house rents, and they reacted in 1827 by trying to have provincial authorities force country dwellers back inside the town.[3] Their excuse for this was that the peasants lacked access to churches and priests and were therefore falling into immorality. Higher administrators and churchmen thought their request unnecessary and took no action.

Several factors spurred the peasant move and acquisition of land. First among these was a particular kind of land tenure contract.[4] The legal ways people relate to the land they cultivate have very strong reverberations throughout a peasant culture. Attitudes toward the care taken in cultivating land, for instance, can depend upon whether it will remain in the family for a long or short period, and whether it can be passed on to future generations. If held for only a few years (or even less, as was true elsewhere in the South of Italy under rental and sharecropping contracts), why should peasants put much effort into cultivating it wisely? The demonstration of this lies in landscapes typified by the appalling soil erosion found in much of the south where people had only short-term rental and sharecropping contracts.

Peasants in Locorotondo who did not already own pieces of land often took them under a kind of lease known as emphyteusis. Under such contracts a larger landowner divided his or her estate among a group of peasants who each took a piece, agreeing to pay an annual rent and transform the land into vineyards within a period of ten years. While they paid the rent and carried out the transformation, the lease was perpetual and could be transferred to heirs. If the peasant failed either to pay the annual rent or to plant the required vineyards, the land, with all improvements made, went back to the landlord. Obviously, this kind of system pressured the tenant to improve the land. Generally, peasant families needed the income from the vineyards to pay the annual rent. This, and the possibility of capturing a piece of land for future generations, inspired careful cultivation.

To realize income, grape growers need a market for fruit or wine. In this respect Locorotondo's peasantry found itself in an advantageous geographical position, perched on the edge of a plateau overlooking the narrow plain that borders the Adriatic Sea. Below, landowners had been in the process of planting olive groves for several centuries, and by the end of the eighteenth the entire lowland zone specialized in olive and olive oil production that fueled both local consumption and a brisk sea trade from the coastal ports. Inland from Locorotondo, in the large zone of Martina Franca, estate-based animal husbandry dominated. Therefore, markets for wine existed to both sides of the town. During the 1870s a vast international market for wine opened up because the grape infestation phylloxera destroyed most of the vines of France. Landowners transformed much of Apulia into vineyards, and at that point neighboring towns, such as Martina Franca, followed Locorotondo's lead into wine production, in part following its model based upon emphyteusis and peasant rural residence. The area of Locorotondo's territory covered by grapevines expanded from about sixteen percent in the early nineteenth century to fifty percent in the early twentieth.[5]

The landowner reaped some short-term advantages from emphyteusis, but to understand these, a little knowledge about local geology and soils helps. The area of Apulia in which Locorotondo lies is a karst. This is an area typified by limestone bedrock covered by a thin layer of red soil. Rainfall in the zone is rather low and what moisture there is drains through the soil and trickles through fissures in the layers of limestone into underground streams that eventually flow out into the sea. This creates marvelous caves with stalagmites and stalactites and interesting karst features such as sink holes, but the thin rocky soil means poor agricultural land. It also means that there are no streams or springs from which to obtain water, and that ground water flows beneath a depth to which wells can be cheaply and easily drilled. Traditionally, sources of water were limited to cisterns kept full through rain catchment, either from the roof surfaces of buildings or from the surfaces of courtyards. Now tanker trucks bring additional water from wells near the Adriatic coast, and the town and many rural hamlets are connected to the Apulian accqueduct, which pipes in cool mountain water from the Appenines in Basilicata.

The improvement of karst land into vineyards in Locorotondo and surrounding towns took an amazing investment in human labor. According to estimates made in the 1950s by an agricultural historian, and according to my informants, there could be considerable variation in this, especially because some land had to be cleared of heavy brush first. On average it took no less than 2,000 adult male work days— almost five and a half years of work—to transform one hectare (about 2.5 acres) from open field to planted vineyard (Ricchioni, 1958: tables 5 and 6). Families labored mightily to gain vineyards, hiring a little help if they could. First they removed the topsoil and piled it aside. Then laborers with picks broke up the underlying bedrock to a depth of about a meter, and removed the large stones, for later use in wall building. Then they created a drainage bed of small stones at the bottom of the resulting excavation. Children, organized in work gangs, hauled soil in buckets from a low-lying karst feature, such as a sink hole, and workers spread it over the drainage bed. Sometimes they also spread a thin layer of clay-bearing yellowish soil over this as a marker of proper hoeing depth for the cultivator. A vineyard was ready to plant when they replaced the original topsoil. The contracts typically specified a ten-year period for transformation, and peasant families went about it row by row of vines.

Obviously this was a very expensive proposition if the landowner hired it done, but by granting the land forever to a highly motivated peasant family in return for an annual rent, he or she solved the problem of what to do with poor local land. The gentleman landowners of Locorotondo were rarely rich enough to plant their own vineyards, and they used what land they held locally for animal husbandry. The richest among them diversified their holdings geographically by seeking large estates elsewhere, sometimes through careful marriage choices that brought rich settlements. Legally, the emphyteusis contract also passed the tax burden onto the shoulders of the tenant, and sometimes, when the tenant could not pay rent or complete improvements, resulted in the return of fully or partially transformed vineyard land to the landlord who thus could reap a windfall with no investment at all.

In the long run, however, it was the peasants of Locorotondo who gained most of the benefits of these strategies. Over the nineteenth and early twentieth centuries inflation eroded perpetual emphyteutical rents to small sums, rendering the land almost rent-free to the tenants and depriving the landowners of much real income. Also, some contracts specified that after several years a peasant family could buy out the contract and become full owners. Many did this.

The nature of land tenure also helps explain why peasants in Locorotondo left the confines of the town walls. The requirement for labor in the countryside was so high that it was more convenient to live on or near fields than to commute to them daily. Hamlets became established in several ways—fathers built trulli for their married sons next to their own, forming family enclaves, and often peasants participating in a major land division ended up building near each other. However, another factor must have entered the decision to live rurally.

The population of Locorotondo doubled over the second half of the eighteenth century, very much stressing the housing available within the walls and immediately outside them.[6] Hard times—this period saw famine, economic crises, war, bandits, and political upheaval—meant that few peasants had the means to build new housing in town, which involved quarrying stone, transporting it on site, and hiring a skilled mason to build walls. (Peasant couples typically received a house, or money to buy one, upon marrying. Few marriage contracts drawn up by notaries during the first part of the nineteenth century describe the building of a house in town.) Trullo construction in the countryside was cheaper because it used locally-occurring unsquared stone, sometimes resulting from the very process of vineyard making, and could be done by peasants themselves under the direction of a master trullo builder. However, in other areas of Southern Italy, equally stressed by population growth, there was no exodus of population into rural housing. This is where the emphyteusis contract became important—it provided an incentive for Locorotondese peasants to live in the countryside, a piece of land upon which to build, and even some stone to build with.

It led to an adaptive strategy. That strategy dictated that the peasants of Locorotondo make their lives in the countryside cultivating small plots for subsistence and growing a crop of grapes each year for market and for home wine production. It probably led to the proverb that says: "If you want to eat bread, stay away from the church bells." The church bells in the proverb symbolize the town with its increased temptations to spend money on things such as appearances and snacks that the peasants of Locorotondo found frivolous. They also symbolized the kind of life led by the town's artisan population, which because it could not produce its own food was generally hungrier and more poorly nourished. Old records show that artisans lived shorter lives.

The values of the present oldest generation of peasants in Locorotondo reflect the adaptive strategy that held during the nineteenth century and the first half or so of the twentieth. These values stressed frugality and hard work above all other things. The purpose of frugality and hard work was to build upon what had been inherited from the previous generation—to "make a step ahead," as a man I interviewed put it. One made a step ahead to provide for the next generation, to set children up at marriage with houses and enough land to begin families. These things were, and to a lesser degree still are, the major criteria for judging success and prestige within the peasant population of Locorotondo. Outside the walls, the peasant population of Locorotondo developed criteria for according prestige to individuals and families that operated in isolation from town ideas that much more greatly valued leisure time and granted highest prestige to those who did clean work such as tailoring, or better, no manual labor at all. In the countryside, peers esteemed the hard working peasant man or woman, but when in town he or she became a *cafone*, a "rube" or a "hick," in the eyes of the town's people. So living far from the church bells also meant living in a more comfortable social world among people with shared values.

As I noted above, Apulian grape growing gained a great impetus from the death of French vineyards from phylloxera, but as the twentieth century began the disease also struck Southern Italy, requiring the replanting of almost all vineyards by grafting European varieties on resistant American root stock. This, along with a late nineteenth century tariff war with France, and economic crises such as the Great Depression in the 1930s, were hard blows for Locorotondese growers, but they did not hold back expansion of vineyards during the early twentieth century.

Patterns begun during the nineteenth century continued until after World War II. Several new opportunities on the horizon in the early twentieth century fostered such development. Now a new possibility for acquiring capital arose: international migration. It was possible for Locorotondesi to go to the Americas, find work, and, using their abilities at working hard and living frugally, accumulate savings with which to return to Locorotondo and buy land. To do just this a small group of local individuals lived for a time during the first two decades of this century in West Virginia working in a coal mine. They were able to return and find enough land to begin new peasant families from the division and sale of a medium sized estate belonging to a local landowner gentleman who needed the money for heavy personal expenses. However, because many of Locorotondo's peasant families already had sufficient land by the early twentieth century, and by Southern Italian rural standards were more comfortable than average, Locorotondese migration numbers were notably less than those of other Apulian towns.

Also, beginning in 1919, major vermouth producers, among them Martini and Rossi and Cinzano, established wineries in Locorotondo and Martina Franca to produce base wine for their white dry vermouth, which is an herbal flavored and fortified wine product used in the United States primarily as an ingredient in martinis. Finished vermouth production took place in their northern plants. The construction of the Southeast Railroad, a private line that connected to the national railroad network in Bari, favored this development. This new market, ready to buy nearly all of the local product, probably helped the area through the crises brought on by phylloxera and the Great Depression. However, it also meant that local wine was transformed into a lucrative product elsewhere, and made the area's grape growers dependent upon a few Northern Italian companies. In 1933 several larger growers assembled a group and formed a cooperative winery—the first in the zone—which had shaky beginnings, but eventually proved a great boon to Locorotondese viticulture. Initially, however, and until several decades after World War II, the cooperative continued to sell base wine to the vermouth companies (Palasciano, 1986, 1987).

The aftermath of World War II brought considerable change to Locorotondo as it did to much of Europe. In fact, in the minds of people old enough to have been through the war, it was the most significant division of time in their lives. The late 1940s and the 1950s were for Italy a time of rebuilding and economic development that resulted in booming industrialization in the north. Similar economic booms occurred beyond the Alps in Germany and in other European countries. An influx of migrant labor from Southern Europe, including Southern Italy, partially facilitated these booms.

Such rapid industrialization had several important consequences in the South of Italy. First, northern industrial production of goods such as clothing, shoes, and tools, drove small artisans such as tailors, shoemakers, and blacksmiths out of the market because they could not compete. The town's artisan population sank into crisis. Simultaneously there arose a demand for a new artisanry that specialized in repairs of such things as automobiles, scooters, tires, and electric appliances. Many among the old artisanry faced changes of occupation, often toward repairing or selling ready-made versions of what they had formerly made themselves, or the prospect of emigration to either Northern Italy or a foreign, usually German-speaking, and not necessarily friendly, environment. Some sons and daughters of the town's artisans were able to complete secondary and university educations and found niches either in local bureaucracies or in teaching positions.

At the same time the landowning gentlemen faced the dwindling of their economic base in medium estate agriculture because of an erosion of agricultural prices, coupled with increases in agricultural wages, and because the passing of transportation and work based on animal power destroyed the market for horses, mules, donkeys, and oxen. Untransformed, thin-soiled, medium-sized estate land in hilly Locorotondo became virtually worthless. Along with the decline of their economic power, this small group of families experienced a deterioration of political power. Power now came to rest in the hands of men from a new, often more highly educated, middle class with professional occupations of various kinds. Many of these were the children of artisans, and a few of peasants.

For a variety of reasons, the peasant livelihood has also considerably changed. First, because of a general proliferation of vineyards in other areas of Apulia where irrigation and therefore better, more reliable, production, is possible, the price of grapes on the market has not been favorable. Vineyards must be replanted every fifty years or so, and low grape prices mean that reinvesting in vineyards is uneconomical. When I first did fieldwork in Locorotondo in 1981 and attended a meeting of the cooperative winery, the aging of the full-time agricultural population became clear to me because the crowd attending was mostly gray-headed. Younger men from the countryside are part-time peasants and full-time workers at other activities. Their wives and daughters have taken over much labor in the fields and vineyards and the family livestock chores. Many men work full time at a job during the day and then return in the evening and spend an hour or two at agricultural work. Part-time farming has become possible because of the system of values about hard work imbued to them by their parents.

Men from the countryside who lead this sort of life have found economic niches in several areas. A few, like a greater number in town, have been able to secure jobs a short bus ride away at a huge steel mill—Italsider—constructed with national government subsidies just outside the city of Taranto in the 1960s as an effort to bring economic development to the south (see figure 1.2). Others have found steady employment in small-scale trucking. By and large the most frequent sort of job found among younger men in Locorotondo's countryside, however, is in construction. There is a new rural artisanry particularly specialized in masonry, reinforced concrete construction, plastering, and tile setting. Every morning a parade of small trucks descends from the Plateau of the Trulli toward job sites within a two-hour drive in the cities of the coastal plain. The new construction artisans of rural Locorotondo are in high demand throughout the provinces of Bari and Brindisi because they put in a hard day's work—again a reflection of values inherited from their highly motivated peasant past. A large expansion of housing in the general area has promoted these changes, and many entrepreneurs from the countryside have been able to build one- or two-man operations into small contracting firms. This has meant a shift of wealth into the countryside and, to a much higher degree than before, the growth of rural political power. This, in turn, has resulted in rural electrification, rural schools, road paving, connection to the Apulian aqueduct, and some amenities like small parks and sitting areas.

Local people have seen much change within their lifetimes. Rural life in Locorotondo is now relatively comfortable and modern. But my adult informants easily remembered chores like cutting and hauling firewood for the hearth and washing clothes by hand with ashes as detergent. In their youth, transportation was by horse and cart or buggy, and most clothing was sewn by local tailors out of cloth loomed at home. The diet consisted of fava bean mush and bread with fresh greens, with pasta reserved for Thursdays and Sundays, and meat served twice a year on Easter and Christmas. What in the United States was essentially a nineteenth-century existence formed the experience of many people in Locorotondo into the 1950s. For them, that existence is "traditional," and most of them greatly enjoy the conveniences brought by change. As an outsider looking back historically it is difficult to perceive what is traditional and what is not. I can see a continuum of change from a time when virtually everyone in Locorotondo lived inside the walls of the town and fewer peasants had land. The traditional existence for Locoroton-dese country people who are still alive is no less the product of changing adaptive strategies than the modern existence of the families I will describe in the next chapters.

NOTES

1. This is clear from two versions of an early nineteenth century land tax roster.

2. This census was taken by the French occupational government as an effort to assess the nature and extent of the kingdom. I analyzed the manuscript copy in the Communal Archives of Locorotondo, which was compiled in 1810–1811.

3. I found the correspondence relating to removal of peasants from the Locorotondo countryside and their relocation in the town in the State Archives in Bari among papers relating to town administration, specifically public works. 1827 *Amministrazione Comunale, Opere pubbliche, busta* 29, *fasc.* 375.

4. This and other generalizations about land tenure in Locorotondo come from analyses I made of contracts drawn up by notaries in Locorotondo from the early eighteenth through the late nineteenth centuries. These contracts are located in the notarial archives in the State Archive at Bari. In Italy, notaries instead of lawyers draw up contracts. (See Galt, 1991a, for further detail.)

5. The first figure is based upon the land tax register (the "Provisory Cadaster") of 1816 in the State Archive in Bari, and the second upon the published cadaster of 1929 (Istat, 1933)

6. There is a population figure from the household census and tax register of 1749, which is kept in the State Archive at Bari, and one from the above-mentioned Census of 1810–1811.

3 / Peasant Lives

AN INTERVIEW WITH MARTEINE

Marteine's 120-year-old trullo lies on a side road in the countryside of Locorotondo.[1] Its walls are a bit run down by local standards, and the furnishings old and worn—they came with his mother's marriage. My field assistant Giorgio and I sat near the hearth as we interviewed the spry, old bachelor who always seemed to enjoy answering our questions about local agriculture, both as it was in 1982 and as it had been when he was a young man. Marteine was 70; he had taken care of his mother until a few years earlier when she had died at 93, and had never married, although he had once been briefly engaged to a woman who he later caught talking to another man. Giorgio and I would stop at Marteine's trullo from time to time to help fill in holes in our understanding of rural Locorotondo in the past, and to benefit from his sharp memory and knowledge of local agricultural matters. This time the conversation got around to abandoned land.

Marteine: There was no abandoned land then, but now yes! That was when people wanted to work. They didn't go off to play soccer, they didn't go to the movies. They always worked; they worked from morning to night. They ate a bite and then put themselves to bed. In the morning they got up . . . and to work . . . until dusk . . . from sunrise to sundown. Now they're all home by five, or they're all in the bars. That's what is wrong with Locorotondo, with these parts.

Giorgio: In your opinion what pleasures did they have, working and working?

Marteine: None . . . you worked. You worked and ate. Also you ate badly. If you could have a smoke with a bit of a cigar or a pipe . . . that was all entertainment that existed.

Galt: But was work a satisfaction in itself?

Marteine: Yes! By Bacchus, it was a great satisfaction! If you could see the men from then. I was a young man, I was; I too hoed. But if you saw certain old men from then . . . of my age . . . dig holes in the ground [from which] to carry dirt from one place to another . . . they were dug well . . . it was the same as if they were cut . . . not even engineers could dig them so well.[2] His grandfather [Giorgio's], the father of his mother, U Boss, he was a professor at cutting dirt. He was a professor. He knew how to cut holes in the earth.

Galt: To dig?

Marteine: Yes, to dig. He worked with a lit cigar. Every blow and fifty quintals of dirt would fall down the way he knew how to do it. It was dangerous when it went down, but he knew how to cut it.

Galt: So you had to have a certain understanding to cut earth?

Marteine: Didn't he go to America?[3] Others went from Locorotondo, two of my uncles. There they dug coal. You measure coal in hopper loads. His grandfather dug two loads, my uncles dug one. That one could fill two, and my uncle [only] one and he ruined his health. He [U Boss] was efficient. He knew how to work.

CHANGING VALUES ABOUT WORK AND AGRICULTURE

Marteine's words are a good starting place for understanding the rural people of Locorotondo, their core values, and how those values have changed. He, like most adults in Locorotondo who were more than thirty-five or forty years old when I first encountered them, talks of one thing as paramount in life—work. From toil comes all other things: food, life's small pleasures, an expanding farm, and most importantly the ability to provide for the family's future. There is a proverb in Locorotondese dialect: "If you want to look good, your bones have to ache." This means that the person wanting prestige stemming from prosperity in the rural community must have earned that prestige from hard work. Sudden wealth of any kind is suspect. Among elderly people, it may even suggest that the suddenly wealthy person has collected a treasure, the location of which has been revealed in a dream by the bandit who hid it, in exchange for leaving an innocent soul—a child—for the devil to take. Such tales abound among the peasant population of Locorotondo. Younger people instead comment that sudden wealth might have come from illegal activities like drug dealing. Nearby Fasano is a crossroads in the Southern Italian drug trade.

With the understanding of the development of Locorotondese agriculture that I provided in Chapter 2, it is not difficult to see why the duty to work is such a central value. Values cannot always be ascribed to material causes. Sometimes free values choices become possible, and there is room for flexibility in the values members of a population hold. I suggest that this might be the case where either there is so much poverty that people have nothing at stake, nothing to channel their choices, or when there is so much affluence that there is maximum flexibility. But in the peasant situation of Locorotondo, which was neither destitute nor affluent, values about work and especially about family were, and still are, strongly influenced by the exigencies of making a living. The adaptive strategy that developed there during the nineteenth and twentieth centuries strongly dictated certain choices. The development of family land could only come about through backbreaking sacrifice by parents who took on land through emphyteusis contracts, or who emigrated for a time, like U Boss, to accumulate enough capital to purchase a few fields. Then family labor could be poured into them to develop vineyards. That process required discipline, saving, and an ability to concentrate all family energy into creating productive resources, and then into production itself. What the peasantry of Locorotondo built through time had to be tended and had to be increased as the next generation came along, and family lands had to be divided to provide for new marriages and households. All of this required disciplined management of resources, both socially and technologically. For instance, soil was managed at the level of buckets full. Terraced fields are common and the owner above had the right by unwritten rural law to recover soil that eroded through retaining walls into fields below.

When I lived in Locorotondo during the early 1980s, some of these values were being called into question because times were changing. The values and way of life that men like Marteine grew up with were threatened by change. At the same time, such people appreciate some of the conveniences, such as refrigerators and cars, that have come with that change. In the past, grape growing and the very small scale agriculture typical of the zone provided a spare living at best. Now many younger men, hardly contented with the frugality of the past, had left the tending of family lands to their wives and to their parents. Younger men, those younger than thirty or thirty-five, faced a dilemma with respect to the lands and vineyards their parents and grandparents had worked so hard to create. Most such men worked elsewhere and not in agriculture, although they often chose to remain residents in the town's countryside. In short, career expectations had changed and many men who had formed families personally experienced such changes. People who grew up expecting to be peasants and agricultural workers found themselves doing things for a living alongside agriculture that took them completely outside the rural sphere.

Work in construction, in trucking, or at the giant Italsider steel mill in Taranto, meant long commutes and real problems when it came to keeping family land in production. Young men and women found themselves caught between the values of their parents, which stressed frugality, hard work, and the conservation of land, and new more generally consumerist values that stemmed from outside sources such as the town and its culture, television, and the city. The temptation to abandon land was powerful, but many kept going, tilling the soil and cultivating vineyards after work and on weekends out of a sense of duty to parents and out of an internalized reverence for agriculture and an appreciation of the values that had made their relatively comfortable lives in the countryside possible. In a real sense, younger men and women in Locorotondo's countryside now ascribe their success in the construction trades to the habits of work their parents taught them, and are strongly aware that those habits came from the agricultural world.

Also there was the sense among them that the agricultural life was a more genuine way of being; this was often reflected to me when people talked about food, always preferring what they could raise and process themselves to what came from the store. "If you make it yourself you know what is in it." Although, as many admitted to me, it was cheaper to buy wine from the cooperative winery than to make it at home (when labor was calculated), most families with vineyards made a year's supply of wine, just as those with olive trees pressed their own oil, those with wheat fields produced their own flour, and those with cows made their own cheese.

RURAL LANDSCAPE AND HUMAN SETTLEMENT

Locorotondo's rural landscape is hilly, densely populated, and thickly lined with roads that radiate from the town center. Smaller connecting roads offshoot from these, giving the map the appearance of a complicated tree root system viewed from above. Mayoral regimes in the 1970s and 1980s busied themselves finding the funds to pave much of this network. The population resides along such roads either in isolated houses, or in small clusters called in the local dialect *jazzèlere*. A *jazzeile* (singular) is a hamlet in which residents own the space between individual houses in common, and rights to use of that space go with ownership of one of the houses. Each such cluster of trulli has a particular story, but many of them originated as newly settled families developing nearby land built new houses next door for marrying sons. Hamlet names often testify to this by pickling the name, or nickname, of a founder. So one finds Agostiniello (Little Augustine), Muso Rosso (Red Muzzle) or Ciccio Pinto (Frankie Pinto). Others are named for saints (San Marco, or Sant'Elia), and others still bear names that suggest a story, usually lost to time— Lamie Affascinate (Bewitched Roofs), or Lamie d'Olimpia (Roofs of Olympia). The hamlets of Locorotondo are notorious for quarrels among inhabitants over the use of the common space and traditional definitions of particular rights. Local

Figure 3.1   A view of the large hamlet of Trito across wide vineyards. Newer rural housing occupies the foreground; trulli occupy the background.

understandings about degrees of quarreling and ways to settle it have developed that probably facilitate living side by side (see Chapter 4). When I carried out fieldwork in rural Locorotondo, the country neighborhoods were well serviced. Electricity extended to all but the most peripheral areas of the municipality. Some hamlets were large enough to support grocery stores, butchers, and bars as well as elementary schools and post office branches. Although few people had telephones in their houses, they were available at stores and bars throughout the territory. Green grocers sputtered about the country roads in three-wheeled scooter carts to sell fresh fruit and vegetables to those who did not grow their own. There was a bus to collect people to go to weekly market on Friday mornings, but this ran largely empty because so many rural households had cars or scooters.

Many hamlets had a public water fountain from which those who had not yet installed running water in their houses could obtain Apulian aqueduct water. Before the extension of the aqueduct system into most of the countryside, the rural population relied upon what water could be caught on the roof and stored in underground cisterns. Roofs, whether trullo style or flat, modern terrace style, had to be kept scrupulously clean for this reason. As demand for water for toilets and washing machines grew during the post-World War II era, it became necessary to truck water from coastal wells up to the cisterns of houses not yet connected to the aqueduct.

Here and there in the landscape there are two- and three-story pitch-roofed great houses that belong, or once belonged, to larger estate owners. These, along with stalls and other outbuildings, sometimes a chapel, and a trullo to house the family of the landowner's estate overseer, or *massaro*, made up the estate headquarters. Only a couple of these larger estates—or *masserie*—remain intact and in the hands of landowning families.[4] Most of the estates have been reduced to the central buildings and a little surrounding land. Occasionally even the central buildings have been sold and abandoned, or used as residences by rural families. The larger estates were much more important in the past, and most of those one can read about in early nineteenth century records have since been divided among peasant small proprietors through emphyteusis or sale. Estate land usually presents an unimproved appearance in comparison to land used to grow crops by rural small proprietors. Most of it is pasture or woods and is thinly soiled with exposed bedrock. Landowners used their estates to breed animals for sale to others, and the loss of any demand for work animals has made estate land worth very little. Sharecroppers cultivate what crops are grown—some wheat, grapes, and other tree crops—in exchange for a share of what is produced and for housing. In only a few cases do the town landowners still go out to their great houses in late summer and early fall to enjoy the countryside, as was the custom in the past.

SMALL SCALE AGRICULTURE THE YEAR ROUND

The present rural population of Locorotondo is not a peasant population in the classic sense of the word. Most rural families no longer totally specialize in agriculture, and most families have at least some members who work for wages in other occupations. I have chosen to use the label "postpeasant" for the current way of life in rural Locorotondo. Now it is common for men to work in construction, trucking, or industry, and for women to tend to the household and to the lighter chores involving cultivation of family land. This has led to what the Italian press often refers to as the "aging and feminization" of agriculture. It has become a national problem in Italy, where food production has long been in the hands of a peasant rural sector. Middle school graduates[5] either go to a trade high-school in a field such as child care or tourism or, more commonly, begin to work. Boys begin an apprenticeship in the construction trades, and girls either find opportunities in local light garment industries[6] or become agricultural workers. Boys and girls who are so employed often hand over their paychecks to their parents. Their income helps support the family, also providing for the settlements children receive when they marry and start their own nuclear families. Despite some notable exceptions to the rule, few from the countryside go on into elite secondary education—classic or scientific high school—and those who do must commute to nearby towns. Locorotondo has an agricultural institute that draws students widely from the region, and even from Third World countries, but does not draw many students locally. Although by Italian law study at all secondary institutions can lead to university admittance, the safest route is through the rigors of attending a classical or scientific high school. Few middle school teachers originate in the countryside of Locorotondo, and few of them give much academic encouragement to rural children.

Therefore, a typical nuclear family household adaptive strategy is to gain livelihood from several sources: children's agricultural or non-agricultural wages, father's employment off the land, and agriculture carried out by men after work and on Sundays, women during the day, and by able-bodied old people who represent the survival of a more purely peasant tradition. Livelihood from small proprietor agriculture comes in two forms: income realized from selling produce, and items produced for household subsistence. According to data I collected in a stratified random sample of Locorotondese rural households in 1982, the average family land holding amounted to between 2.2 and 2.3 hectares (1 hectare = 2.47 acres). This is a tiny amount of land in comparison to an American family farm, to be sure, and reflects the fragmented and generally poor nature of Southern Italian agriculture, even in a zone rare for its population of small proprietors. Moreover, household land is typically fragmented into about three separate parcels, sometimes at considerable distance from one another. Such amounts of land supported peasant families, who supplemented their farm income with wage agricultural labor as late as the 1950s. But as wants and necessities of life increased in the decades that followed, while prices for grapes became less favorable, a purely agricultural existence on "handkerchiefs of land," became untenable. Now, with a few exceptions among a handful of entrepreneurial younger men, who one way or another seek to farm larger areas of land, full-time agriculture is reserved for those in their later years.

About a third of the agricultural land surface of Locorotondo is in tree crops—intensive agriculture. Fifty-eight percent is planted in wheat and other grains, and the rest is in wood lot, pasture, or meadow (ISTAT, 1972: vol. 2, fasc. 74, table 19). Tree crops include fruit orchards, olives, and vineyards, the latter accounting for almost three quarters of this category. There have been marked changes in land use since the early part of the century when 53 percent of the land was in tree crops, mostly vineyards (Calella, 1941: 113). This reflects the crisis of local grape growing and the expense involved with replanting vineyards after they age beyond useful production (about 50 years). Grape growing and wine production in Locorotondo is threatened. Unfortunately, this comes at a time when the local cooperative winery has managed to earn the Italian wine pedigree "Locorotondo White" (Locorotondo Bianco) for wine produced from *verdeca* grapes locally grown, and succeeded in marketing the wine throughout Italy.

BOX 3.1—RECIPE FOR FAVA BEAN PUREÉ.

Dried favas can be found in good Italian grocery stores or sometimes in health food stores. They must first be husked using a sharp, pointed knife, although it is often possible to find them pre-husked. Place several cups of them in a saucepan and cover them with water, adding two or three small, peeled potatoes. Boil the favas and potatoes until soft. Add a little salt to taste, and about a half cup of good olive oil (extra virgin, if available). Beat the favas and potatoes into a pureé with a wooden spoon, adding, if desired, some morsels of leftover bread, or some boiled greens, and more oil for flavor.[7]

Three crops have been, and largely still are, the basis of Locorotondese peasant agriculture: grains, fava beans, and grapes. Of the three, favas have assumed less importance because after World War II and the social changes it brought, the local diet changed. Before that time fava bean pureé, eaten with olive oil, flavored in various ways with herbs and cheese, and accompanied by fresh vegetables and bread, was the basis of local rural fare. It was a diet lacking in variety, but it was not a bad diet when there was enough food for a family. Favas, which are high in calories, when eaten with bread, provided all the necessary amino acids, and fresh vegetables, fruits, nuts, olive oil, cheese, and nuts provided vitamins and fats. Meat was reserved for Christmas and Easter. Country families ate pasta, often made at home with whole wheat flour, on Thursdays and Sundays. The post-war decades brought greater exposure to broader and more urban food habits and a greater craving for meats, both fresh and processed. This, in turn brought a greater reliance on the grocery store and the butcher, necessitating greater income.

Even so, many country families still produce substantial amounts of their own food. The average rural household in my sample survey produced 6.6 quintals (.73 tons) of grain, mostly milled and stored in local flour mills and then withdrawn for family use—a flour banking system. Similarly, the same rural households averaged about 9.5 quintals (just over a ton) of olives, most of which were pressed for oil to be used at home. Out of the 127 families interviewed in my sample survey, 81 produced grapes, and of these, 55 sold the bulk of their production either to the cooperative or to private wineries. The rest produced only enough for home wine consumption. The average household sold 27.8 of the 34 quintals of grapes it produced and retained the rest for home wine making. Other crops commonly grown include garden vegetables, almonds, walnuts, figs, cherries, and other fruits. Except for cherries, which some see as a possible replacement for grape growing, all these are grown for family consumption.[8] A little over a quarter of the households sampled in the survey also kept a cow for milk, typically raising and selling a calf every year. They sold their milk to local dairies, but retained some in the household to make cheese, and neighbors without livestock often bought fresh milk for the same purpose.

Agriculture in rural Locorotondo is still alive enough that one is strongly aware of a yearly cycle of production. The agricultural year ends and begins anew in mid-July. Traditionally rents on land were due on July 15 after the harvests of grain and fava beans were in. Other legumes and vegetables were also harvested during this month. Farmers plow their grain and legume fields and give vineyard soil a final churning before the upcoming harvest. They plant new vineyards during July and August, so in the past this was the time to transport soil to transform fields into vineyards.

Since the 1960s country people have used rototillers to turn the soil. Before then the typical small proprietor family relied upon the large hoe (*zappa*) for cultivation. A hoe in southern Italy must not be confused with an American garden hoe, which is, in comparison, a very light implement. The hoe is a potent symbol of peasant status in Apulia. A man choosing to follow a peasant worker career is said to *andare a zappare*, "to go hoeing," as opposed to, for example, choosing a career in one of the construction trades. The Locorotondese hoe weighs as much as five kilograms (about eleven pounds). It has a broad, sharp bit the size of a shovel blade, and a short wooden handle. It is the chief earth-moving hand tool of the region; shovels are rare. Small proprietors (who typically did not own draft animals) used the hoe to till the soil. The ability to handle the heavy hoe, and the weight of hoe a man could handle, contributed to the reputation someone of Marteine's age had as a worker. Men would suddenly challenge each other in the midst of a vineyard to see who could hoe the farthest in the shortest time. Those with larger fields and draft animals used the Mediterranean scratch plow—a sharp metal point mounted to a heavy wooden stock—to till the soil.

The rototiller was a welcome innovation because it provided the very small scale agriculturalist of the region with a cheap means of tilling large areas of soil without hiring labor. As more men sought jobs in non-agricultural work, the labor saving qualities of the rototiller probably allowed for the persistence of local agriculture. The machine also allows more frequent tilling in vineyards and this extra soil aeration and weed control increases production. A rototiller can even be hitched to a little wagon and used for small scale transport. Lastly, the rototiller, although a chore to use, especially in Locorotondo's rocky soil, somewhat alleviated the back problems suffered by old men, who developed curved spines from a lifetime of chopping the soil with the short-handled hoe.

Soil tilling continues through the month of August, along with vegetable and fruit harvesting. The latter provides work for agricultural workers, mostly women, who work in truck gardens down along the Adriatic coast. August is, however, a bit more relaxed—several harvests are in and the grape harvest has yet to begin.

Everyone looks forward to the Festival of San Rocco held mid-month, when many relatives and friends who have emigrated to Northern Italy or across the Alps return during their yearly vacations. The town fills with people from both urban and rural neighborhoods who socialize, march in processions, eat, listen to band concerts, watch bicycle races, enjoy the amusement park, and admire fireworks. September is still somewhat slack. Oats for fodder need to be sown as do lupino beans. Those who have almond trees harvest and then prune, and olive trees need pruning. In preparation for the impending grape harvest, home wine makers clean the great ceramic jars, some as much as five feet tall, in which fermentation takes place. Some rural neighborhoods in Locorotondo, and several neighboring towns celebrate major saints' festivals during this month and people travel around to them.

October is busy. First comes the *vendemmia*, the grape harvest. Grapes must be cut from the vines (typically a woman's job). Men carry them in polyethylene tubs (big baskets were used in the past) to trucks or three-wheeled scooter carts parked at the roadside for transport either to the cooperative or to the family wine-making facility. Depending upon ripening times, the harvest can consume the first half of the month. Home wine making takes place simultaneously. A person walking through a rural neighborhood can smell the heavy sweet odor of grapes fermenting and can sometimes hear the fizzing of it coming from open *cantina* doors. Most families make two kinds of wine. The first, a lighter variety meant for drinking during the cooler winter and spring months, is directly fermented from must pressed from the grapes. The second is fortified with grape must that has been

Figure 3.2   A worker returns to where women are cutting grapes to refill his tub for a return trip to the roadside.

Figure 3.3   A young woman tends the fire under large copper cauldrons where grape must concentrates into a thick syrup used as an additive to increase the alcohol content of wine.

boiled and concentrated so that the wine develops a higher alcohol content and will last through the hot summer months without spoiling. The grape harvest means heavy work, but that work is alleviated by joking and pranks in the fields.[9] After it is over the vineyards are given a rototilling. October is also the time to begin sowing the next year's fava beans, grains, vetch, and other fodder crops.

In November more sowing takes place and around the middle of the month olives ripen for picking. The local olive harvest lasts into early January and the olive harvest below on the Adriatic coastal plain lasts through March. Households harvest their olives with family labor (often female) and take the olives to one of two cooperative mills to press oil. The coastal harvest creates a demand for female labor, and labor contractors, who are rural residents of Locorotondo, gather up many adolescent girls to work. This opportunity for work, seized by girls to earn money for their trousseaus at marriage, has long existed in the zone, and elderly women remember going down to the olive orchards to stay many weeks while the harvest went on. Now motorized transportation makes daily coming and going possible. In early December, on the Metaponto plain near Taranto, the orange crop ripens and the contractors round up Locorotondese girls for that harvest as well.

An Italian proverb says, "By Saint Martin's Day [November 11], all must is wine," and around that date families sample the new wine. Shortly after that, as December begins, it is time to clean up the vineyards for the next year. Husband and

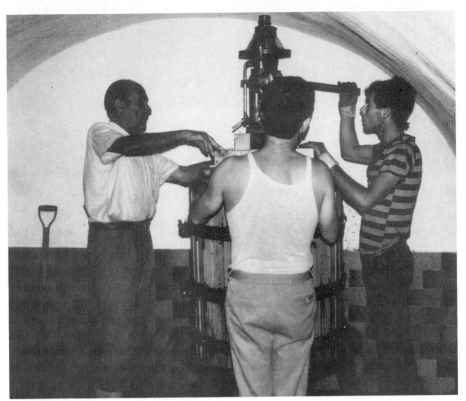

Figure 3.4   Men tend the wine press as they make wine in the home cantina *of a local grape grower.*

wife teams see to pruning each vine and gathering the cuttings. Depending upon the amount of land a household owns, the winter pruning activities can last until the beginning of February, and vineyard chores occupy people during the winter months more than anything else. Most Locorotondese vineyards are cultivated so that vines grow on wires stretched taught between concrete posts. A few are still cultivated with the older system by which vines grew separately, their fruiting branches propped up by forked sticks. Before rototillers, men hoed such that each vine grew from the middle of a square depression and the whole vineyard looked like a big waffle from a distance. Winter pruning is accompanied by a good churning of the soil with the rototiller. March is the month for spreading chemical fertilizer, for grafting new vines, and for forming depressions around free standing vines with the small hoe. These depressions, like those in the old "waffle" style vineyard, help funnel rainwater to the plant roots during the growing season. It is also time to prune olive trees and get garden vegetable seedlings started for later transplanting.

   In April, as the growing season begins for grapes, copper sulfate must be dusted

Figure 3.5   A man using the heavy local hoe in a demonstration of how old-fashioned waffle-surfaced vineyards were formed.

on the vines to prevent downy mildew, a deadly fungus disease. Grain fields need weeding. Halfway through the month, garden vegetables go into the ground, as do chick peas and lentils. Female agricultural workers find employment in coastal truck gardens planting vegetables. Spring continues into May, and fava beans, which look like large lima beans, ripen in long pods. People harvest some to eat fresh or cooked in a delicate soup. They are sweet and good eaten raw. The rest lie in the fields to dry out for summer harvesting. Animal fodder crops like vetch are ready to harvest. In the vineyards women gather to do the green pruning, which consists of removing some leaves and the ends of growing shoots to concentrate sunlight and nutrients in the fruit that will develop. While women do this, men rototill another time. Those few who still breed goats and sheep do so now to produce lambs and kids in the fall.[10]

June comes, and men again spray copper sulfate on the vines and make sure the fruit-bearing shoots of the vines are tied to the wire supports. Grain is ready to harvest at the end of the month and this process continues into July when threshing takes place. The field work involved is currently done by hiring a neighbor with a small mechanized reaper-tier that ties sheaves of wheat or barley. Women gather these and artfully pile them into shocks that look like little huts in the field. Wheat fields in Locorotondo are much too small for the combines used in larger estate

Figure 3.6   A man wielding the locally-evolved pruning knife. These have been replaced by commercially-made pruning shears.

areas of Apulia. Before combines, the grain harvests to the north near Foggia and to the south in the Salentine Peninsula created a high demand for field labor. Both men and women would travel to those places to work for wages in the hot sun. Men worked with the sickle to harvest the wheat and women followed behind gathering it into sheaves. This is an aspect of local migratory labor that has completely disappeared. Favas left in fields to dry in May are ready to harvest in July. With the harvests, the agricultural year ends. In the past, this was the time when debts were due and rents on the medium estates became payable.

In this chapter I have described the postpeasant, as well as the traditional peasant, way of life in Locorotondo. The tasks involved were, and still are, organized among the members of nuclear family households. The structure and atmosphere of families in a place have a great deal to do with what those families must do, especially if making a living is a family matter, not merely a matter of individuals earning separate wages or salaries. The next chapter will examine rural family and extra-family organization in this light.

NOTES

1. Because I promised my informants anonymity when I interviewed them, I have called the man in this interview Marteine instead of his real name. This, like all the interviews translated for this book,

tries to accurately capture the flavor of the dialogue, hence I have not edited it extensively, and I have inserted explanatory footnotes.

2. Marteine refers to soil quarries that were excavated in low spots in the landscape from which soil was imported to vineyards under development (see Chapter 2).

3. Giorgio Cardone's grandfather, nicknamed U Boss (the boss) emigrated, with a number of other Locorotondesi, to Century, West Virginia, after World War I with the intention of making some money to buy land in Locorotondo to supplement what he had inherited. Like many Italian emigrants then and now, he had no intention of staying and returned with his family to settle into the local peasant lifestyle.

4. The larger landholdings in the territory of Locorotondo must be considered medium-sized land holdings in comparison to some of the vast estates of thousands of hectares that have existed in other parts of the region of Apulia.

5. Schooling in Italy is compulsory only through middle school.

6. Such industries sprang up during the 1970s as an answer to the increasing militancy of unions in the garment industry in the North. Local garment making factories subcontract work from northern firms and can get away with paying lower wages, sometimes avoiding paying benefits that are theoretically part of the rights of workers under Italian law. This is possible because of the lack of effective unions in the south, and the greater flexibility of the southern political systems with respect to enforcement of regulations.

7. Small numbers of people of Italian, Greek, and Middle Eastern heritage suffer from a deficiency of the enzyme GGPD, which causes anemia when they eat raw fava beans or inhale fave plant pollen.

8. There is successful cherry growing in neighboring towns, and several people in Locorotondo have experimented with it as a way of keeping land cultivated that is cheaper to plant and maintain than grape growing.

9. This is somewhat comparable to the joking behavior that Brandes describes as typical for the Andalusian olive harvest, although the content is less sexually charged (1980, Chapter 8).

10. There is no longer much market for wool; there are few shepherds; livestock raising time is concentrated on cows; and goat skins are no longer used as receptacles for olive oil or wine, as they were earlier in this century. Raising these animals has become a thing of the past, except for the odd household that likes a little goat milk flavoring in the cheese it makes.

4 / Men, Women, Work, and the Rural Family

THE MAN WITH THE SHOVEL, THE WOMAN WITH THE SPOON

The older way of life in Locorotondo demanded tight family organization around the tasks necessary to make a living from agriculture and to provide for a family's

Figure 4.1 Large trullo with a hamlet in the background. Note how both grapes and fruit trees are cultivated in the same field.

future. Fathers managed family holdings and the labor that went into them, but in Locorotondo there was a strong sense of teamwork between men and women. They often made decisions together. There is a common local proverb that says, "The man with the shovel, the woman with the spoon." Although, as I wrote in the last chapter, men rarely use shovels in Locorotondo, the proverb figuratively expresses important attitudes about the roles men and women should play in carrying on the business of the family. This is an example of a proverb that seems to have an obvious meaning, but that can be misinterpreted if not carefully placed in context. It may seem to mean that men do outside work such as manipulating dirt, and women do domestic work such as cooking, and it could be used in conversation to mean something like that, but this does not exhaust its importance as an expression of folk wisdom. In particular, women's activities are not confined to the house. In Apulia, unlike certain other areas of Southern Italy (Sicily for instance), women do agricultural tasks alongside men, both on family lands and for wages. Each agricultural task has a division of labor according to sex—work involving heavy lifting or the manipulation of heavy tools falling to men. There is a man's hoe—the *zappa*—and a lighter woman's hoe—the *zappeletidde*, used in lighter gardening chores. Picking olives or fruit and cutting grapes fall to women and transporting the produce across the field to trucks to men. Pruning is a man's job, but gathering the pruned branches and grape stalks, which people use in the hearth for cooking, is for women. In family field chores there is a strong sense of team work—men say they feel lost without their wives, and often daughters, out in the fields with them. There is, however, the sense that more skilled tasks—pruning, or overseeing the making of wine, for instance—go to men because they feel more suited to them. Of course, during the two world wars, many men were absent from rural Locorotondo, and often all agricultural chores fell upon women. Many older women have wielded the heavy hoe and have done other viticultural chores to keep the vineyards going, or have had to plow.

Obviously, then, the shovel and the spoon do not merely represent field and domestic work. Rather, the folk selected them for this proverb because they are roughly the same shape, but different in size and function—they are the same, but different. This proverb is a key symbol for the Locorotondesi because it pickles in a few words the idea that gender roles are complementary, and it is used in that context. More accurately its meaning is that men should carry out what is expected of them, as should women, and as counterparts they will carry the enterprise of a family along. This does mean that men should *primarily* be responsible for agricultural decisions and business outside the household and that women should *primarily* be responsible for household chores and child raising, but more deeply it means that in the fields men should carry out tasks defined for them by the cultural division of labor and so should women. More broadly, they should work hard and well together; neither should be a *cazzecarne*, a term for a lazy person that roughly translates as "meat-butt." This strong value that women should work alongside their husbands in a team contrasts strongly with older attitudes about female employment in other social classes in Locorotondo where the ideal was that women be at home.

The importance placed upon the husband/wife team is an artifact of adaptive strategies carried out by the peasantry of Locorotondo. To capture land in the zone, families had to mobilize savings and labor and pour them either into buying land, or transforming it into vineyards under emphyteusis contracts. Both approaches required maximizing family labor, male and female, young and old, either to work for wages, or to work family land, sometimes under deadline, as in emphyteusis contracts requiring that vineyards be created over the space of ten years. The ideal was that wives worked only in family lands, but family members saw, and still see, their potential earning power as a reserve from which to meet needs for cash. Middle-aged women I got to know in 1982 had grown up expecting a life of hard work in the fields and embraced the idea.

When we first met them, Giuseppe and Angela Palmisano were in their forties and had four children, two girls and two boys. Angela minded the house and worked in the family fields like most Locorotondese postpeasant women. As I will discuss in more detail below, boys must be provided a house when they marry, and girls a trousseau of clothing and linens. By the mid-1980s, it appeared that the elder girl, Graziella, then in her mid-twenties, would not marry. The younger girl, Anna, had married and lived with her husband in a neighboring town. Her needs were settled. The eldest child, Giovanni, had not yet married, but probably would soon, and the youngest boy, Domenico, still attended elementary school. Giovanni and Domenico would need houses, and the parents had decided to build one for Graziella as well so that she would be taken care of. This meant constructing two new houses on inherited land and eventually remodeling part of the parental house for Domenico because he was the youngest. The need for income mobilized the entire family to go to work. Little Domenico spent the days of his summer as a helper in a travelling market clothing stall, and his mother returned to work in coastal truck gardens with a labor contractor—something she had not done for many years. This supplemented the steady salary brought in by Giuseppe, the father, as a caretaker at a local school, the income produced by Giovanni as a tile setter, and that earned by Graziella, who worked in a small factory. Most of this income was pooled toward household expenses and toward funds for building the houses, much of the labor for which was also supplied by family members. When we returned in 1986 everyone seemed stressed by new higher levels of work outside the household, and this was on top of the work they had to do in family fields. But there were already fruits from all this work, and the family proudly led us on a tour of the new houses being built a short distance away.

MARRIAGE SETTLEMENTS

The peasant population of Locorotondo perpetuated itself by setting marrying couples up with all they would need to begin a household—a house, a woman's trousseau, furniture, tools, and land. This is a general ideal in rural Southern Italy, but one not always realized, especially among populations where there are few families who own much land.[1] There is evidence, for instance, that among landless agricultural worker populations in Southern Italy, people marry younger and more casually than among small proprietors who have property transfers at marriage at stake (Arlacchi, 1980: 215). Locorotondo's patterns reflect those of at least one other small proprietor population in that the processes leading to the formation of a new household through marriage were traditionally, and to an extent still are, slow and circumscribed with rules.[2] The principle seems to be that the more there is at stake in terms of property when parents set up a new household, the more care is taken about mate selection. This care becomes culturally elaborated.

Although land is no longer crucial to the postpeasant rural existence, it helps supplement income, and receiving a mortgage-free house at marriage is a real boon to a marrying couple. Besides their economic value, the items of property that change hands in a marriage settlement have strong symbolic value. They reflect family prosperity by their number and quantity. Following the custom of the countryside with respect to marriage, settlement also emphasizes a family's continuing attachment to that way of life.

Custom in Locorotondo demands that rural men be given a house by their parents upon marriage. This custom continues to be followed, as the example included above shows. The urban Locorotondese is more likely to have to rent a house or to shoulder the burden of a mortgage to buy one. Typically, a rural house is built using family labor with the help of professional builders when necessary. Since so many of rural Locorotondo's young men are employed in one aspect or another of the building trades, they often have enough expertise to build their own houses, and sometimes exchange labor when they need skills other than their own.

Figure 4.2 A new rural house belonging to a factory worker who moonlights as a plasterer and cultivates vineyards on the side. Note the fancy balustraded staircases. The interior floors are made of polished red granite.

They also have connections that allow them discounts on building materials. Sometimes this results in the use of very fancy materials. For instance, there is a house, built by an Italsider worker who moonlights as a plasterer and cultivates family lands, that has polished red granite floors of the sort that would only be found in the United States in an older bank. Even those who do not work in the building trades can supply manual labor, and this "sweat equity," to use the modern American term, helps keep costs down. This was also true in the past when trulli were built. The change is that not so many men in the past understood the mysteries of trullo building and more direction from a master *trullaro* was necessary. Now rural houses are built with cement blocks and reinforced concrete, and their construction requires less art and skill than the construction of walls from irregular unmortared stone. Only a few men in the 1980s had the skills necessary even to repair trulli, and almost no one could build one using old methods.

Youngest sons inherit their parents' house upon marriage, and this often involves a remodeling to fit two families. In one case, for instance, the parental couple built their house with a basement left for the most part unfinished. They moved into the upper floor. Now the basement serves as storage, and cooking facilities have been installed because it is cooler to cook and eat there in the summer. It was constructed with the idea that upon his marriage, the youngest son would receive the upper story and the parental couple would move down into the basement after some remodeling. Such planning is common when houses are laid out, and sometimes loosely filled doorways are constructed in walls and plastered over in the eventuality that rooms will be added on. This follows the pattern set with trulli, many of which grew from two or three room dwellings to complexes of rooms that grew almost organically during the years. Traditionally, inheritance of the parental house meant that the youngest son also inherited many tools, furnishings, and other household items, and this compensated for not receiving the new house older sons got. With more modern concerns for new and fashionable items this is no longer a great advantage, especially as a younger son and his wife are more likely to face caring for aging parents than other children because of their nearness.

Marriage settlements also bring land—in essence, the peasant means of production. Both men and women receive land, and ideally they bring it to a marriage in about equal amounts. The passage of land between generations often operates in several stages as children marry, and then again when parents have retired from the fields. Nowadays, use of land is bestowed at marriage and no legal contract is drawn up until parents concede all of their land upon retirement. Until the introduction of social security benefits initially during the fascist era, and more fully after World War II, married children gave their parents a maintenance allowance consisting of grain, favas, oil, wine, and the other necessities of life, in equal shares, after the latter had conceded their land. Now the state, with old-age pensions, has taken over from families some of the function of taking care of the aged, but children still provide parents with some home-grown foods, especially wine. Since most men are not full-time farmers, land supplements family income, but can become a burden to keep cultivated. It does have a symbolic value, however, and its inheritance links the present generation with the generations past who captured it. Recall Marteine's strong feelings about land abandonment. Also, a piece of land inherited at marriage can be earmarked for the construction of houses for boys.

Women receive a trousseau when they marry. This consists of sets of linens, both for the house and for personal use. Until the last several decades, the trousseau was mostly home manufactured and decorated with embroidery and lace work by young women before they married. (Early in the century, most peasant households even loomed their own cloth.) Now parents, together with their daughters, buy most of the items that go into it. The size of the trousseau was and is a point of envious comparison, and people talk about the number of "cloths" (*panni*), meaning especially bed sheets, involved. This number has grown steadily through time: three sheets, was an average peasant trousseau during the nineteenth century, and this grew to six between the world wars, now twelve is common. Women are also expected to bring the bedroom furnishings and kitchen utensils. (Men bring the rest of the furnishings with the house.)

Both in peasant times, and recently, providing marriage settlement property created hefty demands on the family budget and parents had to manage carefully. In the early 1980s they continued to expect unmarried children to turn the greater part of their earnings over to their father. From this he would dole out allowances for incidental expenses, and use the rest to meet family costs. However, independence from land and greater freedom from parental control with respect to employment gave modern teens and unmarried young adults higher degrees of independence, and tension sometimes resulted from conflicts among family members over the custom of pooling earnings versus keeping them individually. In particular, jobs in small garment factories removed some country girls from parental control, or from the control of the farm labor recruiter (who also acted as a chaperon), and ideas about retaining more spending money were diffusing among some Locorotondese daughters by 1982.

COURTSHIP AND ENGAGEMENT

Although new ideas about youthful behavior were diffusing among Locorotondo's country hamlets in the early 1980s, most parents still exerted tight control over their children's relationships with the opposite sex. In the countryside there were no casual intimacies between young women and young men that did not have marriage implications. The more urban ideas "boyfriend," and "girlfriend," although familiar from American situation comedies (especially "Happy Days") rerun over Italian television, were alien to country families and in fact could only be translated into local parlance by using words meaning "engaged to be married." However, patterns of courtship and engagement have loosened considerably in comparison to the peasant past.

Courtship, engagement, and marriage in peasant times were tightly governed by rules. The middle-aged to older adults I knew in rural Locorotondo had grown up under that system. Truly arranged marriages, in which the individuals being married had absolutely no say in the matter, were probably rare. However, many informants talked about marriage in the past as more a matter of contracting for property than an affair of love or affection. In practice, in the more purely peasant culture of the past, and to a certain extent in the recent past, parents cut short relationships they did not think were advantageous to their children's futures. Such decisions involved property settlements to be transferred at marriage, to be sure, but also the personal qualities shown by the prospective mates children chose. Here, for both sexes, hard work, frugality, reliability, honesty, and health probably outweighed qualities such as looks as criteria for choosing a mate, both for parents and for children. Affection might be hoped to develop with time, but in pre-World War II engagements, the couple's behavior was tightly chaperoned and men and women had little opportunity for intimacy before marriage. Marriages formed on-going enterprises that, alongside providing companionship and reproducing society, provided families with a living. Marriage was as much about work as it was about affection.

Because families guarded the reputations of their daughters so tightly, opportunities for young people to meet were few. Often it was the girl across the hamlet that a man selected, but several contexts made it possible to meet young women from some distance away. On Sundays much of the rural populace converged upon the town to go to Mass and to make purchases in the weekly market held there. Here there was an occasion for unmarried people to at least catch each others' glances. Parents with daughters held dances in their houses with the hope of interesting young men in them. They held these on holiday occasions, such as Carnival, or on birthdays. Young men would range over the local territory, and after the diffusion of bicycles among the peasantry, into neighboring municipalities, looking for dances. A man who served as dance master rigidly controlled behavior, and because trulli were too small to admit many boys at once, a small crowd would mill about outside waiting for an opportunity to enter.

Once a young man had become interested in a potential fianceé, he would begin to approach her slowly. Most often this took the form of hanging around outside her gate, gradually moving a little closer over a period of days or even weeks to attract her attention. She might reciprocate by puttering about in the trullo courtyard when he was around, and gradually move toward the gate. Sometimes one of them would accompany these maneuvers with notes secreted in cracks in stone walls or even obligingly delivered without a stamp by a rural postman. Gradually they would begin to talk through the gate. Another tactic for a young man was to strike up an acquaintance with the father or brother of the girl who interested him, and gradually come to the point of talking to her that way. Obviously entry into the household of a neighbor was much easier than approaching a distant stranger, and this probably accounts for many marriages made in the immediate neighborhood. Being seen *talking* was key at this stage of courtship, and the neighborhood described two people who were interested in one another as "talking together." So potent a symbol was this that if a woman, once engaged, was seen having casual conversations with other men, the engagement might be called off because her loyalty to her future husband was suspect. Several men I interviewed had, indeed, broken engagements for this reason, although blaming the women involved may have been as much an excuse for rupturing the relationship as a reason.

"Talking," if mutual interest continued, led to steps toward an official engagement. It provided a period, sometimes several months long, for parents to send out feelers about the family of the man interested in their daughter if they were strangers or only vaguely known. In particular, brothers, who usually had wide networks of acquaintances through work connections, made inquiries about family reputation and wealth. It was in their direct interest to help sisters find good husbands because the general rule, although sometimes violated, was that girls in a family be provided for at marriage before boys. Parents could gauge the suitability of proceeding further with the match based upon reports about the qualities of the potential spouse and his or her family. The suitor, after having asked the girl, formally asked her father for her hand. This often involved the girl inviting her suitor into the house to speak directly to her father. If he approved, he would invite the young man and his parents to a dinner where negotiations about property began. The young man also gave his prospective bride a gold neck chain, engagement rings only becoming common after World War II.

Disapproving parents tried to discourage their daughter from "talking" with the interested young man, but this did not always work to cool their mutual interest, and there was always the danger of an elopement. Elopements consisted of the couple running away and spending the night together. Even if it did not lead to a sexual encounter, this act compromised the honor of the young woman and forced an engagement and early marriage. Elopement reflected badly on the parents because it showed that they could not manage the situation, or perhaps that they were too rigid. Elopements also happened when an engaged couple could not stand to wait any longer, often because of the period during which marriage goods had to be accumulated. Marriages resulting from fleeing together were marked negatively by the church, which required that they be celebrated in the basement chapel of the church of Saint George in Locorotondo instead of at the main altar.

Generally, however, families were happy to marry off daughters because unmarried they were seen as a problem. There was always the worry that a woman who aged without marrying would be seen by the community as undesirable or lacking chastity. As elsewhere in Southern Italy, the rural community placed great emphasis on female virginity at marriage. Indeed, on the morning after the wedding night, the mothers of the new couple inspected the sheets from the marriage bed expecting to find telling signs that the marriage had been consummated and that the bride had been a virgin. Unlike certain other zones, however, it was not the custom in Locorotondo to proudly display the bloodied sheet in public. The dialect is rich in proverbs that express concern over the marriage of daughters. For instance, "Daughters are like I.O.U.'s, the sooner you pay them off, the better"; or "Boy: one builds a house, girl: the house falls down," said upon the birth of a baby.

Engagement lasted as long as was necessary to accumulate the items necessary for the settlement and generally until after the fiancé's military obligation was met. "If he isn't ready for the King; he isn't ready for marriage," an old proverb went. Young women started as girls to accumulate and embroider items for their trousseaus, and as they did, they thought about who their husbands might someday be. (There was even a girl's method of divining the occupation of her future husband by leaving the contents of an egg suspended in a glass overnight and reading the shape it took.) The major item was, of course, the house and its furnishings, and this could take a period of several years to obtain.

Rules bound the engagement period tightly. The young man was to eat at his fianceé's house each Thursday and Sunday, no more and no less (these were the nights that pasta was served). Another family member chaperoned the couple at all times. This, of course, meant that intimate conversation between them was difficult and several older couples I interviewed complained that they had only gotten to know each other after they were married. Sometimes it was possible to exchange a few words away from a sibling or a parent, but rarely. A couple seen alone together by gossips risked their reputation and that of their families. An old man, who had married in 1933, explained to me that he had been engaged for six full years and that during that time he and his future wife had never walked together alone. Rules also specified that certain gifts be exchanged at Christmas, New Year's, Palm Sunday, and Easter between engaged people. The new relationship between daughter-in-law and mother-in-law was marked with the gift from the former to the latter of a large frosted dough ring that had an egg, attached with dough strips, baked whole in the shell on it.

The marriage itself was spread over two rounds of festivities separated by a week. The first, the *matrimonie*, was a dinner celebrated with the relatives of the couple a week before the actual wedding. On the wedding Sunday, there was a religious ceremony in church and a buggy drive back to the country hamlet from town. Along the way, friends and relatives hung out quilts and bedspreads to celebrate. That night another dinner, known as the *sponsalizie*, took place. Family members came to these dinners, where meat was served, and brought modest gifts of crockery or tableware. During the wedding night that followed friends pulled pranks, such as lowering a tied and howling cat down the chimney, and serenaded the couple. Serenades had to be reciprocated immediately with an invitation into the house for wine or liqueur and sweets. Somehow the couple also found the time to consummate the marriage. There was no honeymoon among peasants, but they were entitled to a three-day period of seclusion after the wedding day. The community, especially the parents of the couple, expected pregnancy to follow marriage as soon after nine months as possible. For a month after the wedding friends and relatives made individual evening visits, bringing small gifts in exchange for sweets and drinks.

CHANGING EXPECTATIONS

With outside influence and less importance given to agriculture and settlement with land as the center of rural life, courtship, engagement, and marriage have changed somewhat, although many parents continue to have rigid expectations about the behavior of their daughters and tend to seclude them. But there are now more opportunities for young people to meet and get to know each other. School, which is now compulsory through the eighth year, is one, as are work situations away from home, such as the small garment factories. There are still country dances, and there is still the market, nowadays on Friday mornings, in town. Many young men and some young women have cars and scooters and greatly increased mobility. It is not unusual on a Sunday afternoon, for instance, to see young country women standing outside their houses chatting with young men mounted on scooters. However, a watchful mother is seldom far away. Still, engaged couples fall under the surveillance of relatives; "like white flies," as one interviewee noted, do rural fiancés go out together alone, at least publicly. The rigid expectations about Thursday and Sunday visits have fallen away, but frequent visiting of future in-laws is expected.

Young people in Locorotondo's countryside are as bombarded as any other young European or American population by highly charged sexual imagery in advertising, popular music, and television.[3] Exposure to urban life through military service or emigration to the north, or to foreign countries, has also introduced new ideas about male and female relations. The young must reconcile kindled wants and desires with their upbringings. It is difficult to know among how many couples, but some pre-marital sex takes place between rural young people both before and after engagement, and certainly with more frequency than in the past. Cars, and the mobility they provide to out-of-the-way places, facilitate secret rendezvous, and it is not unusual to find discarded condom wrappers in abandoned trulli. Sometimes parents hurry marriages because of pregnancy. It is at least the case that parents complain about it, and older people especially point out that if "the boat is going to sea early," there is little reason to be married at all. They do not cast lost virginity so much in a Christian moral light as a sin, as they see sexuality as making marriage a special relationship that is diminished by having sexual experience beforehand.

Young men find themselves caught in a bind. Having a reputation with women on the one hand builds male reputations in peer groups, but on the other, since young men watch out for their sisters' marriage choices, it may get a fellow labeled as a poor marriage prospect. One recently married acquaintance said, "Whatever you do, you falter"; young men who do not attempt to find sexual encounters, he continued, are labeled as "too flaccid," and those who do get called "bad flesh." Young women face a double standard declaring that if their transgressions become known they will not easily find a mate. Old expectations do not quite hold, new ones have not solidified, and sexuality causes tension.

Since the 1960s the celebration of marriage has become molded more to national custom, with a large church wedding, photographs, movies, and an enormous wedding dinner. This is very expensive and the bride's parents pay for it. The wedding dinner is now a restaurant affair that lasts several hours and contains many courses. The *spumante* flows. (Wedding dinners account for much of the country business local restaurants have, because going out to eat, except perhaps for a pizza, is alien to local ideas about the purity of food.) Many friends and relatives attend, and the expense of the celebration is somewhat compensated by the gifts they bring, which now include household appliances, and television sets. Afterwards, most couples embark on a honeymoon tour of great Italian cities.

CHILDREN

In peasant Locorotondo children were an asset. Five or six children were average for a family, although not all survived to adulthood. In pre-World War II Locorotondo it is likely that one in seven children died in the first year of life.[4] Intestinal or respiratory diseases accounted for most infant deaths. Although worse infant mortality ratios are recorded for poorer areas of Southern Italy, that of Locorotondo is probably high enough that parents worried about the survival of adequate numbers of children and produced many so that some would survive. From my sample survey it was clear that most women married in their mid-twenties, and men in their late twenties and early thirties. This relatively late marriage age for women suggests that to produce five or six children, little constraint was being exercised over conception. That generation of Locorotondesi was definitely pro-natal, and mostly left family size up to fate. Children, as I have noted, began productive work at an early age, both aiding on family land and bringing in income. Many children meant that the family had to work very hard to provide for their marriages. But it also meant that children brought in income that went toward their own marriage settlements and those of their brothers and sisters. An ideal family managed to save and take advantage of opportunities to expand family land holdings so that children could be provided for. Uneconomical medium estate land readily found buyers among the peasantry, and over the years allowed peasant households to expand.

Between the childhoods of middle-aged adults and those of their children there has been much change in child raising practices. Old ways could be quite harsh. Fathers and mothers were stern disciplinarians and physical punishment that modern Locorotondesi think abusive was not uncommon. Fathers beat disobedient boys with sticks and belts, and sometimes restricted their movements by tying them up. Children learned quickly that disobedience to parents brought swift punishment, and learned to bend to their parents', especially fathers', will. There was no back talk. Accounts I have heard stress that dishonesty in particular was subject to punishment, especially when it endangered family reputation, as, for instance, in the case of a child caught stealing something from another family. When contemporary adults relate such experiences from their childhoods, however, they do not do so with bitterness toward their parents. Rather, the sense that parents punished children to socialize them for their future lives comes across. Harsh punishment toward children does not seem to have been arbitrary or capricious or perpetrated out of frustration.

Some of this sternness carries over into the present, although not in such drastic forms of physical punishment. Both the psychological social worker employed by the municipality and the archpriest noted to me that rural parents had the reputation of being harsher with their children than town parents, and both complained, from separate points of view, that rural families lacked affection. Of course, both kinds of helpers were most likely to see problem cases, and neither is of rural origins, and they may have exaggerated, but from personal accounts, I think it is true that Locorotondo's adult generations in the early 1980s had been formed in families where parents tried to inculcate in children a respect for hard work and parental authority, perhaps at the expense of emotional development. There was also little parental interest in schooling, except in a few notable cases.

However, this is not what I observed in the families with children my wife and I visited during our 1981-1982 stay. We had, instead, the strong sense that parents were rather permissive with their children and generous and affectionate toward them. Families now produce fewer children—modern completed family size falls, on the average, between two and three children. One theory that comes up in discussions about these locally widely-noticed changes is that prosperity in the countryside has led parents to want what they could not have as children, both materially and emotionally. Another is that more permissive child rearing is necessary so that individuals develop greater personal autonomy than past generations had so as to cope better with a more complex world. Both are reasonable ideas.

A change that has paralleled this one is that modern parents, where they can, speak to their children in Italian instead of dialect. Elementary school teachers I interviewed claimed that few children came to school anymore who had difficulties with Italian. Rural Locorotondo is less a closed world than it used to be—many parents work outside it and have to deal with people on a daily basis in Italian, even in nearby work situations in Apulia. They realize that Italian spoken at home provides children with a head start at school. Exposure of children to television also helps. Some teachers now actively foster some activities in dialect with the hope that it will not die out with this generation of children, and so that they can better talk with grandparents. Parents, according to teacher informants in 1981, also helped children with homework more than in even the recent past, and followed their progress in school. They were concerned, however, that their children learn practical things to be able to deal with the world of work, rather than seeking higher more intellectual education. Children who grew up during the 1980s will be different kinds of people from their parents.

OLD PEOPLE

Respect toward older people is a central value among rural Locorotondesi, a value that is in some ways the mirror image of the value, already discussed, of providing for children when they marry and establish new households. Under the peasant regime, aged fathers and mothers deserved respect and deference from their children because they sacrificed to provide trousseaus, land, and houses. These attitudes had not changed in the 1980s, although one might hypothesize that greater independence from the land and the old family agricultural way of life will modify them. The principal change in treatment of the elderly that had occurred within living memory was the establishment of social welfare systems that replaced some family functions in providing for the subsistence of old people. Before the coming of social welfare during the fascist era, and the consolidation and improvement of the system during the decades following World War II, all care of old people and provision for them fell to families. Married children shared the burden of providing food and drink for their parents through a practice called *mantenemènte*— "maintenance." This practice has considerable historical depth. I have found eighteenth-century contracts that refer to it among peasants who produced their own livelihood. Of course, a monthly cash allowance from the government, even if meager at times, made this less necessary, although many parents in the early 1980s demanded smaller amounts of provisions so that they could eat "genuine" foods and drink wine without the preservatives put into it by the cooperative winery. Most old people, if able-bodied, find it hard to leave the land totally behind and so continue at least to garden and therefore produce some of their own food.

When the youngest son marries, he brings his bride to live in a remodeled part of the house he will eventually inherit. This means that parents are likely to rely heavily upon this son and his wife for help as they age, and the daughter-in-law/mother-in-law relationship in this instance can be especially conflict ridden because of the nearness of the older and younger couples. This is somewhat alleviated when the time comes that either both parents begin to need greater amounts of help, or one of them, especially the mother, dies, leaving the other alone and helpless. Under such circumstances, old people go *mési mési* ("month by month") among their children, both male and female. If children live at a distance, this involves month-long visits to their homes. If children, as in the case of youngest sons, live close by, care may be provided from door-to-door without actually moving the old person. There are rare cases where both parents need care, and to spread the burden somewhat they circulate separately among children. This custom continued to be strongly felt in the 1980s. For sons, the bulk of care provided for old people fell on wives. This made the daughter-in-law a key figure in the welfare of older people, and certainly entered into consideration when, earlier in their lives, they contemplated their sons' marriage choices.

Childless couples, or men or women who never married, used a form of adoption to assure some care when they grew old. This they called *servetutene*—literally, "servitude." Such a person might choose from among nieces or nephews an individual to treat as a son or daughter. The chosen son or daughter would move in and provide help and companionship in exchange for a marriage settlement. This eased the burden of his or her own family, especially if there were many children.

NEIGHBORS

Neighbors in rural Locorotondo can be important, and people are well aware of this when they talk of the relationships that are important to them. On the other hand, the neighbor relationship, especially in a hamlet where shared resources are at stake, can be a source of problems and tension. Some neighbors are kinsmen, but others are not, and many people live at a distance in the countryside from their kin, especially if they do not live in a hamlet. In peasant times, as more recently, people called upon their neighbors for many reasons and tried to maintain good relationships. For instance, help must be mobilized during calving, and households with cows turn to neighbors to provide it. The neighbor relationship is so intense that neighbors exchange services in washing and preparing one anothers dead for funerals. Here, as in other cases, a proverb underlines the importance of the relationship. People say, "Even the queen is the subject of her neighbor," and this emphasizes the need to submerge one's own pretensions in favor of cultivating neighborly relationships.

However, local people remark upon the intensity of bad relations that exist in Locorotondo's hamlets. Quarrels between hamlet neighbors center upon several things, among them disagreements over how to use the shared space and facilities between the houses, real or imagined slights to courtesy, and conflict between households arising from quarrels between children. As I noted above, space in a *jazzeile* between the houses, and any facilities such as cisterns, threshing floors, or grape squeezing facilities fall under common ownership between inhabiting families. Although eighteenth- and early nineteenth-century contracts spelled all these rights out, more recently they appear to have been transmitted only on an oral basis. Common decisions about modification or use of communal hamlet space or facilities must be made unanimously. In essence, the hamlet is not only a neighborhood, but a common farmyard owned among independent farmers. Independence on the one hand, and common ownership on the other lead to conflict, especially when two parties need the same resource—a threshing floor, for instance—at the same time. Such conflict can cause, or serve as an excuse for, hostility between individuals and, by implication, their households. Some features of this communal farmyard have fallen into disuse—grape squeezing facilities, for instance—but there continue to be hamlets that are notorious for squabbles among neighbors.

The rural communities of Locorotondo have a four-level classification system for conflict situations and some ways, which do not always work, of dealing with that conflict to restore greater harmony. Hostility between members of a hamlet affects relationships between kinsmen and other neighbors and disturbs local harmony. Since neighbors need each other, this reduces security. I would ascribe the concern neighbors show with categorizing hostility and with trying to heal it to this fact. "Faking" is the first level of conflict. Someone who has been slighted, or who feels treated unfairly, might say nothing to the injuring party, in the interests of maintaining harmony in the neighborhood. Once, when our son had been subjected to verbal abuse by a harried neighbor, and we felt slighted and angry, a neighbor quoted the proverb: "The person who understands better fakes it." This means that it is better to ignore slights and wait for them to blow over. (It is also applied to soothe the ruffled feathers of a daughter-in-law who feels she has been mistreated by her husband's mother.) The proverb and the behavior it describes allows slighted individuals to think of themselves as wiser in the situation.

The next level of conflict between neighbors recognized in the system translates as "each at home." Here a conflict situation is more apparent in the behavior of those involved as public conversation is reduced and visiting at home ceases. Beyond this, hostile neighbors are said, at the next level, to "say 'Hi' and walk on." There is no public conversation and relations have been reduced to muttered greetings. Finally, the most intense level of conflict is total avoidance, labeled "no longer looking at each other's faces." In such a state estranged individuals might go out of their way to avoid even passing each other. All but the latter state might heal with the passage of time, but in the 1980s there exist rifts in the countryside of Locorotondo that will probably never heal.

There are some natural leaders in Locorotondo's countryside, some of whom people think of informally as "hamlet head." In the post-World War II period, local political parties sought out and adopted such widely respected, charismatic men as go-betweens in the local political clientele system (see Chapter 7) and to some extent this institutionalized what had been a purely informal function. Informally, such men often served as peacemakers trying to talk estranged neighbors into making up, and in so doing trying to heal rifts in the hamlet level social fabric. One way of doing this was to try to convince one injured party to give in, to "put himself under" the other one. In long term rifts, the original issues involved had often lost relevance and giving in sometimes involved the loss of nothing more than a little pride. Palm Sunday offers an opportunity to make peace without even discussing the quarrel. Kin, friends, and neighbors exchange a blessed olive twig on this holiday to show their mutual solidarity and respect. Everyone takes branches of olive to be blessed at church on the morning of the holiday. On Palm Sunday, one party in an estranged relationship can offer a twig to the other. If it is accepted, the quarrel ends automatically with no further discussion. Otherwise, it continues as before. The little ritual of the twig provides a way for people to test whether enough time has passed since the original affronts for people to forgive and forget. Often friends and neighbors urge the exchange.

RURAL SYSTEMS OF BELIEF

Except for a tiny handful of Mormon converts, all Locorotondesi are Roman Catholics. However, rural people in particular have a religious and magical culture that differs from formal aspects of that Christian denomination in several ways, although many rural people—women especially—go to Mass, and almost everyone goes through the official sacraments—baptism, first communion, the wedding Mass, and the funeral—that accompany various stages of life. Although I was able to collect much ethnographic interview material about religious and magical belief, it is difficult to say, without the ability to read minds, how wide among the rural populace such beliefs were in the early 1980s. There were certainly skeptics about both standard and folk Catholic beliefs and about the effectiveness of magic. Most of what I will describe below lives on among older people relatively unchallenged. Changing times, lessened isolation, and more education has made inroads on these beliefs among younger people, but I did encounter some people in their twenties and thirties who held most of the beliefs I will describe.

As in much of Southern Italy, women serve families as the liaison between the everyday world and the transcendent world of the church. It is they who are more likely to go to Mass; it is they who serve more generally as a repository of beliefs; it is they who bear most of the brunt of mourning upon death, at least in that they, unlike men, must dress from head to toe in black for varying periods depending upon the closeness of the relative who has died. (Older women turn to wearing black in their forties or fifties, and, because either their close relatives, or those of their husband, continually die after that, they rarely wear colored clothing again. Men show mourning only with a black cloth covered lapel button or a ribbon.) Many men do not go to weekly Mass. Some who might not go to Mass, however, will take part in outdoor processions in honor of a saint.

Much of rural religiosity, especially as practiced by older people, revolves around saints. Saints are associated with locales, churches, and towns. Most everyone bears the name of a saint, and name days are celebrated in families. Particular saints can help the living with specific problems. Paramount among these is sickness, and the medical saints Cosmo and Damian (patrons of neighboring Alberobello), and Locorotondo's patron saint, San Rocco, are widely venerated as healing saints. Besides saints, the cult of the Virgin Mary is quite important in

Locorotondo. In Apulia there are several pilgrimage sites associated with the discovery of an image of the virgin in a well, often by a child who has miraculously survived after having fallen in. Locorotondese peasant women take organized bus trips to such sites to pray for favors. The Catholic church has a rich symbolism associated with holy personages, and this is particularly evident in the statues of saints and the Virgin used inside the church at their altars and outside during processions held on locally celebrated saints' days. Saints' statues are carried in procession. Sometimes people will make a vow to a particular saint in exchange for a cure for disease, or another favor, and it will consist of walking barefoot in procession under the saint's statue (which usually has an ornate hollow base). Saints who are not celebrated with festivals in Locorotondo, but who appeal to people, Saint Martin, for instance, have major festivals in neighboring towns, and people travel to them, to Martina Franca in this case, both for recreation and to walk in processions.

BOX 4.1—THE TALE OF SAINT MARTIN

Saint Martin was good. Saint Martin was too good. Well then, he had a sister, Saint Comasia. This sister, Saint Comasia, was in love with a young man, this sister. And Saint Martin didn't want it. They had neither a mother nor a father [that is, he was head of the family and responsible for her]. Saint Martin said, "Well," he said, "I am going to carry her with me on my horse at all times." And he put the sister on his horse and he didn't let her get off so she couldn't put horns on him [that is, betray his honor by eloping with the young man]. Well, she said, "I have to pee," said the sister. "Go on!" he said, "I don't even want to let you go behind those bushes," he said. And the sister said, "Throw a rock, you'll see there's no one in the brush." Her fiancé was in those bushes. And what did the fiancé do? He had a bird with him. The sister had told him, "Go hide in there." She told him [Saint Martin], "Throw a stone into the brush, you'll see. So Saint Martin threw the stone into the brush. He [the fiancé] let the bird go, and it flew away. "Well," said Saint Martin, "if there are birds in there there can't be a living soul," [and he let St. Comasia go into the brush]. Then after the sister returned to poor Saint Martin, she got up on the horse behind him. The further they went the heavier she got, the further they went the heavier she got. He said, "Goddamn it," he said, "what an ass I've been, what an ass I've been!" said Saint Martin. "Well," he said [to his sister], "go away I don't want to see anything more of you."

So then he set out wearing a cape, Saint Martin did. While he went he saw a poor man who was shivering all over. He said, "Give me a piece of that cape," he said, "because I'm cold." So Saint Martin gave him a piece of the cape and clothed him. He came to another poor man—this other one also shivered—and he gave him a piece. It went that way until he remained naked and had dressed all the poor men . . . Saint Martin. He went around bare-assed until he felt cold and then he made the sun come out. That is the origin of the Summer of Saint Martin.[5]

The important saints have tales associated with them and those tales, at least among the older, more illiterate country residents, often have little to do with official church versions of those saints' lives (see Box 4.2). Often the tales stress points of purely local morality rather than of any sort of universal Christian significance. In several cases the tales seem to also function as explanations of symbolic elements found on local statues of the saints. The story of Saint Lucy, who was martyred by having her eyes plucked out, revolves around why she is shown in paintings and statues with her eyes in their sockets as well as in a dish held in her hand. Her father became angry with her because she "talked" with a boy he did not approve of and tore out her eyes, but they magically grew back each time he did it. The tale cautioned parents not to be too inflexible about their children's marriage choices. The local story of Saint George revolves around the saint's being able to kill the dragon because his horse put a hoof on the beast's tail. No one's horse had done that before, and so no one had been able to slay it. The earliest local statue (late sixteenth or early seventeenth century) of the saint in the town's oldest church, La Madonna della Greca, and the statue in the pediment on the church of San Giorgio's facade, both show the horse this way. These tales show that, until recently, the rural folk operated somewhat on their own in a religious world in which explanations by priests were in Italian, an alien language, and rituals were carried out in Latin.

Local folk do not view priests with automatic benevolence. There is a proverb, for instance, "Priests . . . black on the outside, black on the inside." That is, the color of their clothing is reflected by the color of their hearts. Also, folk wisdom considers meeting a priest in one's path first thing in the morning as a bad omen that will make many people turn around and go home. Such peasant attitudes about the clergy are not rare in Southern Italy, where, in the more distant past, they or the institutions they belonged to acted in ways similar to large secular landlords and noblemen. The revolutionary processes that occurred in the early nineteenth century and again at Italian unification in 1861 involved the placing of limits on church power wielded on the basis of large amounts of land. More recently, the church has been complicit in the rise of the Christian Democratic party, and many Southern Italians have memories from the immediate post-war years of priests distributing packages of spaghetti in church in exchange for promises to vote for the party. In general, many rural people, especially men, suspect the priesthood of hypocrisy with respect to several matters, especially the vow of celibacy and in matters of charity. On the other hand, people drop general prejudices toward certain clergy-men who are more popular than others. More importantly, although Locorotondese rural men may avoid the organized aspects of religion they claim to believe in God; but because they have never directly experienced divinely supernatural things they hesitate to describe ideas of Heaven or Hell. Theirs is a concrete world view in which personal experience is the basis for knowing things.

Some people do directly experience the supernatural, however, and several informants claimed direct observation of ghosts, rather than church teaching, as the basis of their belief in life after death. Ghosts arise in cases of suicide, which in the country, unfortunates sometimes commit by jumping into a deep cistern and drowning. A ghost then "comes out" and haunts the vicinity of the cistern until the time that the person was fated to die a natural death. Many people have seen ghosts, or know people who have, although one man told me that ghosts are more rarely seen nowadays because everyone whizzes about in the countryside in cars. They appear in strange forms such as miniature cows, hoof beats with no visible horse, and cats with flaming tails. The psychiatric social worker in Locorotondo reported to me that a client had seen a female figure over the mouth of a cistern beckoning her to jump in—a pathological ghost image as seen by a depressive. Most people express no particular fear about ghosts, however, because once the observer realizes that what he or she has seen is a ghost, it immediately disappears.

Another being that many experience is the *ajure*. This is a form of incubus or succubus—a creature that comes in the night and sits on peoples' chests rendering them immobile so that they cannot even open their eyes. While she sits there she tangles her victim's hair and pinches his or her body leaving bruises the next morning. Unlike, classic incubi and succubi, noted from Medieval witchcraft lore, the *ajure* does not attempt to have sexual intercourse with the man or woman she visits. The *ajure* is also particularly fond of horses and, in former times when people kept them, would go out to the barn and braid their manes. When an owner mistreated a horse, the *ajure* would beat it even more during the night as a kind of perverse lesson to humans. Those plagued by the *ajure* attempt to get rid of her attentions by sitting on the toilet with food and inviting her, in a rhymed spell, to eat with them. This she finds disgusting, and she leaves. I have the impression that many in Locorotondo's countryside have experienced her visits, or some physiological "night terror" phenomenon that they associate with her. In conversation, people who described the phenomenon talked as though they were surprised that I had never had a visit from the *ajure*.[6] Another being that is part of local lore, but rarely directly experienced, at least nowadays, is the *monachidde* (little monk), an elf-like creature who helps in the stalls by feeding and watering the horses while the master sleeps.

Indirectly, at least, people also experience the workings of both God and the Devil. The latter is vaguely blamed for damaging storms, and the crosses and other symbols painted in whitewash on trullo domes—many are now faded—were once probably painted to provide protection. God, on the other hand, is thought to punish the living directly for their transgressions. There are, on the one hand, human curses that, if launched by a genuinely wronged individual, strike their victims. The texts of these curses often include invocations of God or Christ, as in: "I want from Christ that what he made happen to me happen to him!" (Others are more figurative, such as, "May the fate of a mouse in a cat's mouth happen to you!") Curses must be uttered by the truly wronged, however, because if they are not they return to strike the launcher. It is but a step from the curse, with its appeal to divine justice, to actual automatic punishment of the wicked by God while they live on earth. This is called, in dialect, *a malapotènse de Digghje*, "the harmful power of God." This is a divine curse, essentially. One of my informants said, "God's harmful power is what will strike a son who, after having been given his marriage settlement, doesn't want to have his mother go month by month with him." God is thought to punish such extreme disloyalty as that with sickness and poverty, or perhaps a shortened life. Curses and God's harmful power protect the weak in rural Locorotondo, especially women who are widowed and alone, and therefore vulnerable, or young women in danger of abandonment by fiancés. The possibility of a fianceé's curse, or perhaps that of her mother, makes young men think twice about casually breaking off engagements. These beliefs concentrate in areas of potential tension—parent/child and male/female relationships—and when widely believed (probably as late as the 1950s or 1960s) certainly operated as social control mechanisms that made people think twice about betraying others.

Rich rural belief systems also included two forms of evil eye and witchcraft. In most places it occurs, harm transmitted by evil eye works through envy. In Locorotondo there are two forms, one in which the envy is unconscious and the resulting harm is usually an intense headache, and another in which envy is actually verbalized by one or more people and the symptoms are vaguer in the sense that they involve bad luck, or financial troubles. The first may be diagnosed and lifted with a ritual involving drops of olive oil in water, but not prevented, and the latter cannot be cured, but can be prevented through the display of amulets like red plastic, or gold, twisted horns, goat horns, open scissors, or horseshoes hung in strategic places.

In the early 1980s there were a few people in rural Locorotondo who considered themselves to be witches, and to whom some of the rural populace turned for curing and protection from harm such as the evil eye, or the spells of other witches. Local belief is that, at any one time, there are seven witches in the general territory, and that they are in league with the Devil, who has given them a magic book and instructions about how to use it. They charge money for their services, and people claimed to consult them most frequently when doctors did not seem to help in the curing of problems. They could also provide harmful magic, even to the point of occasional death spells. Another service is providing love magic for use in situations when a young woman desires the attentions of a young man who does not appear naturally interested. Fear of this magic has caused mothers in rural Locorotondo to warn their sons about consuming liquids—coffee or wine—in households with unmarried women in them.

This description does not totally exhaust the magical and supernatural belief system of rural Locorotondo.[7] There are strong ideas about fated injury and ill omens, for instance, but for the sake of brevity, taken together the magical-religious system makes up a derivative of Roman Catholicism, but with a high degree of inventiveness, carried out among the rural folk of Locorotondo, who hold among themselves a culture that is related to, but varies from, that of other kinds of people in Locorotondo.

NOTES

1. The reader might compare the situation in Locorotondo with that described for Stilo, Calabria, by Pitkin (1985: 19–22), where young people were usually forced to marry with rather little and to make do. Pitkin describes a family that originated in Stilo and migrated to an area in central Italy. After much hardship and hard work, this family manages to provide its children with houses.

2. The comparable population is that area of the Region of Calabria known as the Cosentino, which has been described by Pino Arlacchi, an Italian sociologist, as being composed mostly of small proprietor families, and as having rigid rules and expectations about marriage (1980).

3. As anyone who leafs through the Italian weekly magazines will soon discover, contemporary Italian popular culture is even more highly charged with sexual imagery than that of the United States.

4. Unfortunately local public health records that survive are spotty and this figure can only be calculated from one year, 1936.

5. This tale, as reported here, is slightly edited from an oral text collected in the field. Note that the

first section about Saint Martin and Saint Comasia has nothing to do with their official lives, as accepted by the church. It seems to be a cautionary tale, like the one about Saint Lucy, mentioned in the text, about the consequences of men being too harsh about the marriage choices of their daughters and sisters. The second part has some reference to the official tale about Saint Martin, who gave his cloak to a poor beggar, who was Christ in disguise. Images of Saint Martin show him giving up his cloak. Here, however, Christ does not enter into it, and Saint Martin ends up riding around the countryside naked on a horse, and feeling the cold he causes the sun to come out giving rise to the Summer of Saint Martin, an expectable warm spell like our Indian Summer, around Saint Martin's day in November. There is an expression in Locorotondo which is "to lead the career of Saint Martin," and people use it to refer to others whose prospects in the world are diminishing.

6. Another population that suffers visits from such as creature with some frequency is that of Newfoundland. See Hufford, 1982.

7. I have written a more detailed article on the topic that makes the point that, taken together, all the local beliefs about magical harm comprise a system for talking about suffering and the morality of victims and perpetrators (Galt, 1991b).

5 / Artisan Lives, Artisan Values

SOCIAL CLASS AND SOCIAL CHANGE IN TOWN

I have already shown how the peasant population changed from being totally occupied with agriculture to embracing a series of new occupations in building, and how this altered rural life in Locorotondo. To look at similar questions, I now shift to the town and processes of change over the three decades before my field study. Here I must confront the question of social class in Locorotondo and how it has shifted alongside local and national social and economic changes. The change is marked. This chapter will focus upon the working classes in Locorotondo's urban sector; the next upon middle and elite classes.

It is often difficult to describe systems of social class as seen from within a complex society because people from different ends of the system tend to see things a bit differently. For peasants, for instance, the old differences between what local elites called the middle bourgeoisie—the higher class based upon professional incomes, as opposed to the agrarian landowners whose income came mostly from estate land—were not nearly as significant as the differences between peasant small proprietor and estate overseer families (*massari*), or between peasants and artisans. Also, to many in the upper classes, peasants were just peasants with respect to their place in the hierarchy, despite differences in wealth or relationship to land among them. In spite of these differences of elaboration and emphasis, it is possible to reconstruct the locally perceived class structure that held in Locorotondo until about 1960, and therefore well within the lifetimes of most adults when I did fieldwork there.

Many people grew up with one set of expectations about their careers and their chances in life and had to modify them as circumstances changed. The old system—which originally had its roots in the early nineteenth century with the end of feudalism—was roughly composed of peasants, artisans, a "middle bourgeoisie" (larger scale merchants, professionals, and teachers), and landowners, in that order. Townspeople sometimes referred to the wealthy landowners as "nobles," but this was figurative; Locorotondo had no real resident nobility. Generally, the criteria that imbued individuals with higher class included wealth, education, clean work (or better, no necessity to work), and having an old family name, in the sense of a long heritage of belonging to Locorotondo's elite. People coming from each group tended to make further distinctions within their group (there was a hierarchy of artisans, for instance), and within groups with which they shared nearness. Thus, the elite groups in Locorotondo recognized the ranks among artisans, their co-residents in the town. Near the upper border of the "middle bourgeoisie" there were those with old family names, and perhaps some inherited land alongside their professions, who approached the landowner families in rank. At the lower end of the category there were those who carried out clean professions that required a certain amount of education—school master, or grocer, for instance—but whose incomes and whose family heritages were not grand.

Over the thirty-five years that separated my fieldwork in Locorotondo from the end of World War II, social distinctions between families and individuals lessened, although hardly did they disappear. Figure 5.1 attempts to illustrate those changes by showing how old categories have become collapsed into emerging new ones. Such diagrams must be taken only as rough models, however, because they collapse the individual realities of people into overly neat boxes. For instance, there remain in Locorotondo people who consider themselves members of the old landowning elite and who continue to behave as such, although that category will fade completely as they pass away. Their parents certainly brought them up to expect to lead upper class lives, but they could not because of broad trends that have made living mostly on estate income difficult. I have tried to diagram what I saw, and what most local people see, as trends in the formation of a new system of classes.

By the early 1980s the old town elite categories had collapsed into a single new elite composed of professionals, bureaucrats, and larger merchants. The old professional classes had children continuing in the professions, and new entrepreneurs involved in retailing had arisen from several sources. Finally, educated children of the old artisan class, as well as some who were not educated, could claim new elite status based on professional, entrepreneurial, or bureaucratic activities. Some of those who had been brought up as artisans, expecting to spend their lives in the workshop, had found niches in a series of new artisan occupations, and some had become factory workers in newly-developed heavy industry at Italsider in Taranto.

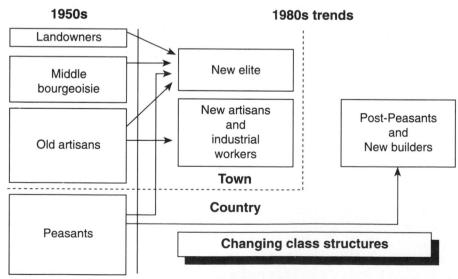

Figure 5.1   A diagram showing the changing configuration of social classes in Locorotondo since the immediate post-World War II years.

On the 1980s side of my diagram I have placed the rural population at a level almost equal with new artisans in town. Such equality is begrudged by people in town, although the urban/rural animosities and prejudices that existed in the past have not completely died out. Many rural people still feel shunned and discriminated against by those from town. Some older people have truly bitter memories of this. But wealth, and to an extent, political power in the rural population, have broken old hierarchical images of country people being lower than working people in town. Also some of the new elite—a doctor, the head of the cooperative winery, and much of the faculty and leadership of the agricultural high school, for instance—come from peasant origins. Some men of rural origins have made their fortunes as construction contractors and have successfully chosen to follow careers in local politics as well. This chapter examines the working people of Locorotondo town within this framework of changing social class structures. The next will examine elites.

A CONVERSATION WITH CICCIO

We sat with Ciccio at Giorgio's kitchen table. Ciccio, then forty-seven, used to be a tailor, but like many in the artisan world of the post-World War II era, had gone on to other things, among them a period of emigration to work in Northern factories. He answered our questions in clear and precise Italian, tinged by dialect only when he imitated someone else who would not speak Italian. Our conversation ranged over many topics. This was one of those happy interviews anthropologists hope for in which each question stimulated a vast flow of information from the interviewee; little follow up questioning was needed. The conversation got around to the artisan world of the immediate post-World War II era, when Ciccio was a young man, and the divisions within it:

Ciccio: The artisan environment was also divided into several categories. Barbers, tailors, shoemakers, and carpenters were the four pilasters of artisanry. There weren't even many plumbers because there wasn't much plumbing. . . . In the artisan world there were elevated categories and lower categories. Herders and cart drivers were on the bottom. (Knifings [among them] were not uncommon.) There were artisans of Series A, Series B, and Series C.[1] Masons were considered below the tailors, barbers, shoemakers, and carpenters. They were "the dusty race," and they were kept at a distance because their trade was little regarded and not considered an art by other artisans. The higher categories were called *li artiri* [in dialect]. Masons were considered manual laborers. Within the big four there were distinctions that were not merely based on skill. The tailor was the highest . . . they considered themselves a step below doctors! The tailor was more highly regarded than the shoemaker. The shoemaker's job was considered dirtier. . . . To marry a tailor had a certain prestige, even though it meant a life of relative poverty. The artisan gave more to others than to himself. Artisans did conscientious work, but this was indirectly against their interests because they didn't get paid for the quality that they produced. And they didn't realize it. They lived that way, "on glory," as they used to say.

Q.   Was this because there were too many artisans?

Ciccio: Yes, there were too many, but there was also too much work. Then there was no competition from factory-made things. Everything was done by hand by artisans. So there was work. Even though his work was considered like that of an artist, his work was simply not rewarded. He had to live on art, and couldn't live on anything else. If they managed to survive and get ahead it was because there were many apprentices. They weren't paid until the age of twenty.

Q.   How did they learn their trades?

Ciccio: They started early. Either you get used to it when you are little, or you never will get used to it. It is hard work that can't be taken up as an adult. They were sent to the workshops because there wasn't any choice. It wasn't possible for the children of artisans to study. Rural occupations weren't admissible. The artisans would not send their children to become peasants, goatherds, or cart drivers. There was never any movement from the center toward the countryside. . . . This wasn't because the peasants were considered repulsive. It is just that there didn't exist any way to become one if you weren't one already in your family. There was no peasant apprenticeship. You're born a peasant. . . .

Q.   Peasants ate favas and more favas . . .

Ciccio: [interrupting and correctly anticipating the question's direction] There was a difference between the peasant and those in the center. Because he produced food, the peasant didn't have as much of a problem to resolve about eating. Since when do peasants buy anything to eat? He produces everything. The peasant never had a problem with eating.

Q.   What kinds of things did artisans eat?

Ciccio: There was generally the first course.[2] In my house this was never missing, but to get a second course was not an everyday thing. The first courses consisted of pasta or beans. It was all bought. Sometimes artisans worked for peasants in exchange for food. This was especially true during the war when even if you got paid in money you might not find food to buy.

Q.   Daily food, what might it be? Could you eat meat and fruit?

Ciccio: No, no . . . now yes, but then you ate meat only on feast days. The most common dish was pasta—it was cheaper. It also filled you up until evening. . . .

Q.   At what age did you start going to the tailor shop?

Ciccio: From the age of eight or nine, but you didn't work that young, you just started going in the afternoon after school. This was to keep you off the street. When you finished elementary school (some didn't) you went to work. They used to say, "It is enough to know how to sign your name when you get married." A worker didn't know how to read a newspaper, he didn't have to know anything but his work. . . .

Q.   Did artisans rent houses?

Ciccio: Yes, it would be difficult to find a property owner.

Q.   Who owned the houses?

Ciccio: Always *that* class [i.e., the elite]. Small scale property ownership only formed later in town. Just in the last few decades. Originally the shops belonged to the gentlemen, but many of them were acquired by peasants for use as a resting place to change clothes when they came to town on Sunday. Now many country people come into town when they grow old and live on their pensions. There are a lot of them up in the park sunning themselves. . . .

Q.   In what year did traditional artisanry enter a crisis?

Ciccio: This happened as the process of industrialization of the whole country proceeded. And with the advance of consumer society. The artisan was not a protagonist in this, the large industrialists were. Ex-tailors work for them.

Q.   In 1950 what stores were there in the urban center? When you were sixteen years old?

Ciccio: No clothing stores at all. There were some in Martina Franca. They also sold clothes in the market. All stores were pretty limited. There were no furniture shops. There were a few shoe stores—most shoes were handmade. . . .

Q.   If we want to put a date on the artisan crisis can we say the 1960s?

Ciccio: Yes, I was a tailor then. In 1960 it was hard to find boys. You had to work alone and couldn't produce much and compete with ready-mades. Later, there was less work. You couldn't satisfy a client fast enough. If you have more orders than you can handle you lose them. It simply wasn't possible to keep up with industrial competition. Working in a factory had more advantages—there was the medical insurance and other benefits. In good tailor work it was all hand work and it couldn't be done by a single tailor without apprentices. The traditional master tailor only did fittings and cutting. Most of the hand work was done by boys. Artisans caught in the crisis led the career of Saint Martin.[3] Locorotondo was the living plant of tailors. There was a super abundance of tailors and they were exported all over the world. Especially to Argentina. They were in the majority here. After midday meal every day the park would be full of tailor's apprentices who would soon disappear into the shops at 1:30. There are few tailors left.

BEFORE THE GREAT ARTISAN CRISIS

Ciccio introduces the changing world of the town artisan. Artisans made up the bulk of the population of town Locorotondo until recent decades, and the values and world view of artisans form a significant part of the experience of many living townspeople of both working and middle class. They were immediately distinguishable from higher elites because they worked with their hands and made things. In the 1950s there were few stores in town—only ready-made shoes had started to penetrate the local market before the World War II. (Used clothing, imported from the United States, could be bought cheaply in the weekly market.) If a peasant wanted a new suit, he took cloth (often woven by one of the women of his household) to a tailor in town to have it made up in exchange for cash or foodstuffs. The elite woman might find a picture of a pair of shoes she liked in a fashion magazine and take it to one of the better shoemakers to have it copied. Her only alternative was to travel to Bari or Naples to find a selection of ready-made shoes. Most hardware used in building—hinges, hooks, locks, keys, railings, gates, and so on—came from local blacksmith shops, as did tools such as hoes, plows, and pruning hooks. Other metal workers made cauldrons of beaten copper for making cheese, and other items, such as weather vanes, cut from sheet metal. Masons used locally quarried stone to build, and specialists among them could carve it skillfully for decorative touches. Locorotondo boasted a cart factory that serviced a wide area in Southeastern Italy. There was also a pipe-organ maker of some renown.

Locorotondo and neighboring towns nurtured craftsmen with high levels of skill, as a visit to the pharmacy on the main street of the historical center of town will show. There the visitor finds a beautifully carved and finished wood-paneled interior with cabinets done in the florid style of the turn of the century. It would rival work of the same period in a large center like Naples or Rome. With high levels of skill went high levels of pride, even in everyday jobs like making hoes for peasants. A proper Locorotondese hoe took many hours to forge and certain blacksmiths had reputations for being able to anneal especially hard and resilient steel edges on the huge iron blades. Peasants liked durable tools and returned year after year to have them sharpened and re-edged.

The artisan world was sharply ranked by occupation. (See figure 5.2.) First came the cleaner occupations—tailoring and barbering—that sometimes meant entrance into the households of the local gentlemen. The world came to the elite; they did not go out to meet the world. Then came the shoemakers, who, though they dirtied their hands with dyes and polishes, gained prestige from working inside sitting. Their shops were also places to drop in and find a conversation. Below them came carpenters and blacksmiths, both highly skilled trades, but ones that meant getting dirty. One blacksmith reported that as an apprentice he had felt self-conscious crossing the main square with dirty hands and face on his way home for midday meal. Then in the artisan hierarchical world view there was something of a gap, after which came the stonemasons who other artisans labeled "the dusty race," or "dusty men," in direct reference to the dirt and limestone dust that covered them as they worked. (Stone sculptors fared a little better because of their artistic skill.)

In the eyes of other townspeople, the lowest of the low among town working people were goatherds and cart drivers, who, even if they lived in town, or on its fringes, spent a great part of their time outside it. Townspeople perceived them as little better than peasants, and as hard drinking roughhousers who resorted to their fists or even to knives to settle differences. There was a tavern on the edge of town

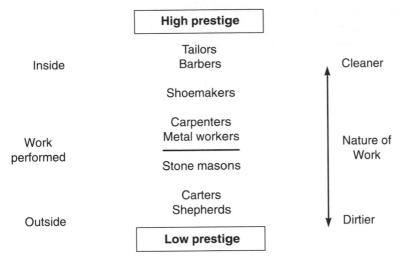

Figure 5.2   A diagram showing the dimensions of rank in the old artisan class. Whether work was performed inside or outside and the degree to which it involved getting dirty had much to do with prestige.

at the major crossroads, where such men gathered. In particular, a cart driver nicknamed "Lo Sfabbante" is legendary for having drained an entire goatskin full of wine in a single long swallow in defiance of a landowner who had denied him and some other carters their customary wine ration after a job was done. Early in the century, before the authoritarian single party politics of fascism set in the 1920s, locally warring political factions used herders and cart drivers as henchmen to intimidate voters during elections. Among peasants, who of course lacked prejudices about people who worked outside, carters and shepherds were not stigmatized. Some also lived in the countryside.

Apprenticeship formed a significant part of the early lives of both men and women from the artisan category. All boys were apprenticed, by no means always to their fathers. The hierarchy of trades influenced parents following other crafts to try to place their sons with tailors, for instance. Parents also apprenticed girls, after they finished elementary school, to seamstresses and embroideresses. The expectation was, however, that after they married they would not work outside the house. Those who married tailors did sewing for their husbands at home, not in the tailor shop. Angelina, a tailor's wife, spoke of having drawn a storm of criticism from other tailor's wives by openly working in her husband's shop. (Her marriage was one of the rare matches between an artisan man and a peasant woman, and she saw the in-groupness of tailor's wives with a certain contempt, and brought to her marriage the rural value about working alongside her husband because it was more efficient.) Apprenticed young women fell under the watchful eye of their *maestra*, who not only taught them their skills, but walked them every day to afternoon Mass. This was one of few opportunities for artisan boys to look them over, make eye contact, and perhaps initiate a future relationship.

The most significant characteristic of this apprenticeship system was that two sets of people formed the characters of young people. These were their parents, with whom they lived, and their master and sometimes their master's wife, under whom they worked, and with whom they spent more of their waking hours. The artisans I interviewed painted their *maestri* as stern figures who were very demanding, but who, in return, inculcated in their apprentices skill and appreciation for the craft. Ciccio recalled an instance when his maestro, who forbade smoking in the tailor shop (for obvious reasons), stepped out for a moment and he furtively lit up a cigarette. Unexpectedly the *maestro* returned. So his boss would not suspect, Ciccio quickly plunged the lit cigarette into his pants pocket, and it burned through to his leg as he fought showing agony on his face. Fear of the the *maestro* was greater than fear of fire. *Maestri* kept a watch over their boys and that attention sometimes extended beyond the shop and its activities to the apprentices' social lives. Many masters did not hesitate to provide what they thought was moral guidance about the company their boys kept, or even about marriage. Sometimes a master would have to retrieve a boy who was truant from the shop—they sometimes snuck away to play cards. There might be physical punishment, and when the boy's parents heard about it they would add to it when he got home, in support of the *maestro*.

Although master craftsmen could be like second fathers to their apprentices, there were commercial forces that could create conflict between them. An apprentice who learned well and quickly was a threat. Once he left the nest to establish his own shop he became a competitor. Some masters tried to stave this off by keeping what they thought were the secrets of their craftsmanship from apprentices as long as possible. Giuseppe, a blacksmith now engaged mostly in assembling aluminum door and window frames, told me that when welding equipment first became available in his master's shop, the latter would allow no one but one of his own brothers to learn to use it.

Sometimes this stimulated the apprentice to adopt devious ways to gain trade secrets. The founder of Locorotondo's organ factory, Francesco Consoli, learned his trade in Turin in a renowned organ maker's workshop where he rose to the position of shop head. The *maestro* was extremely jealous of his methods for tuning the pipes and would not teach them to his workers. Instead, he preferred to lock himself in a windowless room while carrying out this significant finishing touch. According to the account by his son in a locally published reminiscence, Consoli, like the Greeks in the great horse at Troy, hid in a chest in the room and observed the whole process through a narrow slit. Shortly after, realizing that organ manufacture and repair little existed in the South of Italy, he packed his bags and established his business in Locorotondo and supplied organs to churches throughout Apulia (Consoli, 1988: 138).

Artisans have the same degree of respect for hard work that exists in the countryside, but it is a different kind of work and values about it were somewhat different. Peasant values stress independence from others and being able to do as many tasks as possible using only family labor, if possible. One might rely upon a neighbor but mostly for favors one could reciprocate, such as helping at calving, lending a hand during the grape harvest, or preparing the corpse of someone who had died. Instead, artisans held utmost respect for expertise and specialization. A blacksmith would not make a copper cauldron; that was the province of the coppersmith. A proverb says, "If you have to get yourself flayed, get yourself flayed by a good butcher." This expresses the idea that good craftsmanship might cost enough to hurt, but it is worth going to the best specialist. Artisans I interviewed contrasted that sort of attitude with the peasant idea of being able to do many things at home. Peasants, in the eyes of artisans, would cut their children's hair and even try to make shoes for them, to save money. Ciccio told me, "Our peasants take care of themselves." For instance, much of the simple furniture— stools and benches—in old trulli were made at home. Artisans, by contrast, turned to other artisans for their needs. Except for tool making, artisans also felt that work for peasants could be done with less refinement than work for town people, especially when it came to clothing or shoes. Some tailors and shoemakers would descend into the countryside and set up temporary shop turning out goods for peasant clients, often in return for payment in food.

Under the old regime of master artisan and apprentices, the number of orders, and the need to make enough goods to sell in the market drove the pace of work. This meant that the shops kept working until the orders were finished and that sometimes meant that apprentices worked beside their master until late at night. Talking to men who apprenticed during the 1950s, I have the impression that there was little leisure, except perhaps on Sundays, and that the day consisted of working, breaking for a family meal at midday, and then returning to work until it was almost time to go home, eat the small evening supper, and go to sleep. The only leisurely moment during the day was at 1:00 in the afternoon when artisans and apprentices gathered in the public gardens for a half hour of conversation. A church bell and the horn of the Martina Franca-Bari bus arriving at 1:30 sent everyone back to the workshops. Twelve-hour work days were the rule six days a week and it was not unusual to work Sunday morning as well. There are common stereotypes, both in Italy and in the United States, about Southern Italians being casual about work, or even lazy. The working people of Locorotondo, both peasant and artisan, negate them thoroughly. Only people in higher classes could afford much leisure time.

As Ciccio tells us in the interview passage, artisans worked hard and cultivated skill, but they were poor. Except for some master craftsmen, artisans struggled. Their housing mostly consisted of small town apartments, usually on the first or second floor of the old buildings in the town's historical center. The old center is small in area—most of it would fit within two rows of three football fields—but the streets are narrow and maze-like and it can house several thousand people. Such apartments consisted of single rooms with an alcove, perhaps, and some niches and closets in the wall. There also would be a hearth and, in the days before the Apulian aqueduct serviced the town, access to a shaft that led down to the cistern under the house from which people drew drinking water. The aqueduct brought water to town early in this century, but not everyone had running water and plumbing until several decades after World War II. Such spaces housed whole families. A local doctor described having to step over sleeping children to get to patients he had been called to examine. Artisans' houses and workshops were cramped and damp, and the same doctor indicated that the artisan categories in Locorotondo suffered a great deal from respiratory diseases, such as pneumonia. Sometimes, especially with stonemasons, this became complicated by breathing dust. Most artisan families rented their houses. Only rarely did houses come as part of marriage settlements as they did in the country.

Figure 5.3   The local Società Operaia, or Worker's Society, a recreational club for artisans that also operates a communally-owned mausoleum in the cemetery.

The peasant diet was monotonous, with fava beans day in and day out, but in general it was healthier than that of artisans, who ate much pasta but did not always get adequate amounts of greens and fruits because, with a few exceptions, they did not produce food. They got by with what they could buy at market or from the local food shops, or with what they could get from peasants in return for their services. They took advantage of what they had at a given moment, and quoted the local proverb, "The rich man consumes when he wants something, the poor man only when he has something." Like the peasants, they ate meat only on special occasions, such as saints' festivals when butcher shops roasted it for the celebration.

There are accounts of hunger, especially early in the century, among some artisans, stonemasons in particular, who would stand outside the doors of the local gentlemen and ask for food in exchange for doing odd jobs (Lisi, n.d.: 1). Although peasants also knew hunger sometimes, the artisan idea of the interior of their houses included shelves stacked high with home-produced cheeses, crocks of oil, sausages, and supplies of grain and favas. Artisans, especially their children, often treated peasants as second class citizens among Locorotondo's working people, but they envied them their self-sufficiency with respect to food. A favorite pastime of artisan children was to descend from town into the countryside to raid fruit trees, especially for figs.

Marriage and family patterns differed somewhat between artisans and peasants, although in both populations parents tightly controlled the behavior of young people, leaving them little opportunity to get to know each other. Young women remained in the house or in the seamstress's shop, only going out to Mass in the evenings and on Sundays. Sometimes parents kept their daughters away from house balconies, and fathers accompanied them to their work places. They expected their children home from the workshops within a few minutes of normal closing time and would come to check on them if they were not. Parents did household shopping and went to draw water from public fountains; they did not send young women on errands. The tailor's wife who grew up in the countryside claimed that there was more opportunity for peasant young people of opposite sex to meet and talk, because country girls had to do more work outside, especially in the walled courtyard in front of the house.

Artisan young people stole glances and exchanged a few words showing interest and intentions on the way to and from church and work. "Pairings," said one of my older acquaintances, "came about, where they were not arranged, by spontaneous germination under the absolute domain of silent but expressive glances." The country usage of hanging about the gate to attract a girl's attention was not possible in town because their mothers kept them away from the house's openings. The narrow, densely inhabited streets of the old historical center of Locorotondo facilitated gossip among neighbors, especially during the warmer months when older women congregated in front of their doorsteps in chairs to shell fava beans or knit. The open dance custom of the countryside, which provided an opportunity for courting, did not exist in town either. In fact, those few more prosperous artisans who owned a trullo outside the town, and used it as a summer retreat, could misunderstand country dance customs. They would throw a party, invite local country girls and exclude roaming country boys, who, to get even, would play pranks on them. What parties there were in town among the artisan categories— Carnival was the main occasion—were get togethers between families behind locked doors for fear that they would be crashed by "hotheads" from among the carters and herders.

Young men, after having expressed their interest to the women they courted through eye contact and glances, made their intentions obvious. Such "declarations," as they were called, often consisted of secretly passed notes. There would often follow a lengthy period of furtive exchanges of conversation and notes—a pre-engagement. Contact was minimal and the couple made every attempt to keep it from both sets of parents. In an interview, an artisan woman remembered that her suitor had taken to going to 6:00 A.M. Mass before work just so that he could pass by her house every morning. She would lock herself in the bathroom, which had a window that looked down on the street, and they would exchange a smile and a word or too this way. Her father would get up early once in awhile to go hunting, and express consternation that she was always in the bathroom at such an early hour.

If she felt agreeable to more serious steps, a young woman first paved the way by asking her father if the suitor could come in and formally ask for her hand. As in the countryside parents might try to put a stop to an engagement they did not like, but this could produce an embarassing elopement. Without quantitative data, the frequency of such behavior is hard to talk about, but some people remembered elopement as a common thing among town dwellers. The face-to-face nature of the town community meant that parents on both sides of a match had an immediate sense about the reputations of the young people proposing betrothal, and about their future in-laws, and the checking that sometimes went on over a distance in the countryside was less necessary.

Although town girls brought a trousseau with them to the marriage, property considerations at marriage were much less a concern than among peasants because very few artisans had houses or land to give their children. Of course those few who had a little property were in a good position on the marriage market, especially if a house was involved, even as an eventual inheritance. What each family would provide for the new household was agreed upon between them at an engagement get-together. A few families provided house rent and free board at the parental table for two years, but this was rarely possible. Some women brought little or nothing to their marriages, but the average expectation in the immediate post-World War II era was a bed, and a chest for the trousseau linens. A trousseau with ten of each major item (sheets for instance) was average in that time. Now brides are expected to bring entire bedroom suites. People laid more emphasis, perhaps, on questions of honesty and uprightness, and upon a reputation as a hard worker. The artisan's livelihood depended entirely upon his skill and dedication to his craft—he usually lacked resources besides his tools. A tailor I interviewed volunteered his classifications for reputations among young people. There were *ragazze da marito,* "girls fit for husbands," and *ragazze con le quali si scherza e basta*, "girls with whom you joke around, and that's all." Then there were *ragazzi da sposare*, "boys for marrying," and *ragazzi che vanno girando e basta*, "boys who roam around, and that's all." Parents would not let the latter sort of young man—with a reputation for drinking, perhaps, or for getting together with friends during work time to play cards—enter their house to ask for a daughter's hand.

The behavior of unmarried daughters was, however, more crucial, and more apt to be controlled tightly by parents and relatives. Even aunts and uncles kept an eye on young women, and the tailor quoted above commented that an uncle might slap his niece if he found her in a compromising situation with a man. If an unmarried woman's behavior involved a violation of standards about curbing sexuality, it led to wagging tongues, lost marriage chances, and the risk of a troubled life. A young man could more easily recoup a shaky reputation. In the historical center, as in the countryside, an engaged woman who was too familiar with a man other than her fiancé—to the extent of conversation that could be judged by the observing community as flirtatious—could easily cost herself the engagement and damage the reputation of her family, including that of any other unmarried women in it. The surveillance and seclusion of women, as practiced in Locorotondo, guarded far more than merely the welfare and reputations of single individuals; it kept whole families from trouble and preserved their honor.

During the period of engagement, which could last several years, contact between fiancés continued to be limited, although young men could now openly visit their fianceés as long as chaperones were present. Sometimes in the evening they would find a musician or two (barbers usually played guitars or mandolins to pass the time in the shop between clients) and romantically serenade their brides-to-be from the street. And sometimes it was even possible to steal a kiss in the shadows of evening streets when no one was looking. Some who courted this way remember the old ways as romantic, but few would trade them for the more open customs of today.

My older town informants saw family as being of paramount importance to them, and gave less emphasis to the neighbor relationship than did people I talked to in the countryside. To dwellers in the historical center of Locorotondo the expression "say 'Hi' and walk on" referred to the normal state of social distance between neighbors, not the alarming state of estrangement it does among country people. In town the two major sources of relationships for men were family and work place;

Figure 5.4   Street scene near the historical center of town.

little brought them together unless they were kin or co-workers. Neighbor relationships were perhaps more important to women who stayed home during the day.
During the summer especially they spent time sitting in chairs in the alleys in front
of their houses exchanging gossip and socializing as they did hand work. But, the
cheek by jowl nature of town living, neighbors stacked one upon another in
two-story buildings across narrow alleys and courtyards, creates, even now, an
atmosphere in which minding one's own business helps prevent conflict. Until the
1960s, when the construction of larger apartment houses on what was then the
periphery of town began, most town Locorotondesi lived in the historical center, or
in the old neighborhoods that grew just outside it. Relatives were never very far
away and could be called upon when help was needed. Since men spent their youths
in tight contact with other apprentices and in an almost familial situation with their
masters, they formed primary friendships in the workshop, and they spent what
leisure they had with work friends or relatives. After hours, or on a Sunday, adult
men might hang around together in the square or the public gardens, play cards in
one of the political section offices, or a wine shop. Typically people gathered in
family groups Sunday afternoons and evenings, and they still do.

BOX 5.1—TETÈ AND TUTUCCIO

In the lore of Locorotondo's artisans and their descendants, stories of witty
and clever townsmen live on. Among them are Tetè and Tutuccio, both
shoemakers, stories of whose exploits and verbal duels during the first three
decades of this century still enliven the conversations of townspeople and the
pages of local publications. We can, thanks to the latter, eavesdrop upon
some of their remembered conversation (Ancona, 1988: 116):

Tetè and Tutuccio, a little inebriated, have left the wine shop at closing
time and taken up a position on a bench in the municipal park. They sit
admiring the view out over the surrounding countryside, trulli shining in the
moonlight.

Says, Tutuccio, "Tetè, they say that the world is round. What do you think?"
——Of course it is round. It is round like our town. Don't you know the
story?
——No.
——. . . Well, here is the story of the earth. One splendid sunny morning, the
eternal Father said to San Pietro, "Dear Peter, With a day like this I want to
create something beautiful. I want to create the earth." "O.K.," said San
Pietro, "but make it good, because man must live there, as half-witted and
weak as he is. If you don't make it good, the poor devil won't be happy. He
won't be happy, and you won't cut a good figure." "I'll do my best," said the
Eternal Father, "but how shall I make it, square or round?" "Better make it
round," answered San Pietro, "then you can turn it around to suit you, and
when it doesn't work well, you can give it a kick and send it to the Devil." So
the Eternal Father formed a model of dirt and rocks, and that model, because

of its form, he called Locorotondo.[4] Therefore Locorotondo was the model
for the earth. The model for the world. What a beautiful thing, Tutù!
——It's a beautiful story, Tetè, but if the world is round, how does the water
in the sea, the lakes, and rivers stay up in the air?
——. . . The hand of God, Tutù, is so large, that it holds up the water, even
the wine."

Artisans staffed the town band, and formed the center of musical culture in
Locorotondo. Many learned a wind instrument to play in the band to earn some
extra money. In Locorotondo this tradition goes back at least to the early nineteenth
century—I have found the document that laid out the rules for the operation of a
band in 1807. In Southern Italy there is great connoisseurship of wind band music.
This tradition has produced some world class musicians.[5] Some bands, and musicians, are regionally renowned, and there are composers of both secular and
religious processional music who are well known among the populace. The two
major contexts for wind band music are funeral processions and festivals. For the
former, the mourning family hires the band to play slow dirges to accompany the
casket and the funeral party up the main street of the town on their way to the church
of Saint George where the priest will say the funeral Mass. Country people in

*Figure 5.5   The Locorotondo town band playing in a religious procession during
Easter week.*

particular have long made a show of this, and Ciccio the tailor described a series of conversations with a visiting police officer, who was staying in Locorotondo during the winter when there are higher frequencies of deaths and funerals. On the first day the officer saw an opulent funeral with lots of mourners, flower arrangements, and the town band, and remarked to his hosts that an important person must have died. The host said that it was only a peasant who had passed away. The officer was astonished at this, and his astonishment grew after several more opulent peasant funerals during the following days. He remarked to his host that the local peasants must be really well-off to permit themselves the luxury of all the flowers and hiring a band. The host explained that "our peasants" make do with little, work very hard, strive for independence, and save much money. The officer then quipped memorably for his artisan audience, "Well then, they skimp on life, so that they can enjoy death!" Notably, to distance themselves from the rest of the population, the highest elites in Locorotondo are said to have hired the band for their funerals to march in the procession, but they would ask it not to play. Not all artisan families could afford the band to accompany their dead up the hill, and one of my informants claimed that it was the case among artisans to attend only the funeral Mass in church, and not join the procession, so as not to miss much work.

The band also plays in processions associated with saints' festivals and, except for the Holy Thursday procession, which recreates a funeral procession for Christ, the music is brighter. In addition to processions with the local band, each festival also includes fireworks, street decorations, concerts by a visiting band, (or for important celebrations like San Rocco, two visiting bands) that plays classical overtures in the main square inside an elaborately decorated and illuminated bandstand. The local artisan population comprises most of the audience for such concerts. Individuals from the peasant and postpeasant population I talked with about music were less interested in band performances and preferred the dance music played at country dances by rural musicians with small accordions.

Around the turn of the century, Locorotondo had a celebrated touring band that was often invited to play in other towns. They even toured internationally, playing in Northern European capitals—once before the German Kaiser. This band was composed of artisan musicians who played under a dynamic leader, Antonio Gidiuli, who, as a young man serving his military obligation in Rome, caught the attention of the Queen of Italy. She bestowed upon him a scholarship to study at one of Italy's most famous music academies. Although there are few alive who heard Locorotondo's great band, memories of something so renowned having sprung from home are still a source of pride to many. Soon after World War II Locorotondo's band and music school declined, and the current town band plays for home consumption alone, but with enormous enthusiasm.

THE ARTISAN CRISIS AND ITS AFTERMATH

Social and economic change brought the artisan world into crisis all over Southern Italy in the late 1950s and early 1960s when competition from ready-made goods of

Figure 5.6   A cluttered hardware and housewares stall during Friday's weekly market.

all kinds made severe inroads in the livelihoods of men and women who previously had supplied most of the simpler needs of the population, and even the more deluxe needs of elites. The working people of Locorotondo mostly had to find new opportunities as a result. Industrial expansion in the North of Italy after World War II, made possible in part with help from the United States, and Italy's joining the European Common Market in 1957, meant a diffusion into Southern Italy of cheap and durable goods produced elsewhere in factories, mostly located in the northern regions of Italy, but also abroad. Little industrial manufacturing existed in the south and this is still the case. Simultaneously, mass media—magazines, radio, and television—containing advertising and consumer-oriented features began to diffuse. This redefined the basic needs and wants of life for southerners of all social classes, and living on the low incomes that "traditional" artisans received no longer seemed very attractive to young men, who, a generation earlier, would have gone directly from elementary school into craft apprenticeships of various kinds.

Into the 1950s the historical center of Locorotondo was a busy workaday place. A shoemaker I talked to estimated that before World War II there had been 111 cobbler shops and that in them as many as 300 people, masters and apprentices, practiced the trade. In that specialization, commercial production began to make itself felt even before the war. There were also high numbers of tailors and their apprentices, and there were tailor shops containing as many as 25 apprentices at a time, although this was not common, and most shops employed one or two. A morning's walk through the whitewashed maze of the old town now reveals only an occasional tailor or shoemaker shop, and whoever strolls up the town's main boulevard passes some ready-made stores like the English named "Man, Lady, Baby Shop," or the elegant boutique a few steps from the public park. What was probably worse for the local artisan classes was the wide adoption of automobiles and scooters. Such means, coupled with frequent bus and train service leading elsewhere, facilitated shopping over a wider radius. From the 1960s through the 1980s cheap department stores, such as Standa, opened in nearby Martina Franca and Fasano. Stalls with ready-made new clothing also proliferated in the weekly market. Hardware stores opened, ending the need to go to a metal worker for many needs. The small and large department stores supplied kitchen equipment needs, making severe inroads, not so much into Locorotondese artisan livelihoods, but

Figure 5.7   A woman in mourning shopping for a plastic tub during weekly market.

throwing whole towns such as Grottaglie, in Taranto Province, which specialized in the production of ceramics for a vast area, into crisis.

Parents and children from the artisan group adopted various adaptive strategies to cope with the changes that took place. Donato, an elderly tailor, and his wife Angelina, talked about the fates of the nineteen men and two women who had apprenticed with him. (The women specialized in sewing pants.) When we spoke in 1981 only three of the men remained tailors in Locorotondo. In the 1970s, another, after having begun as a tailor, successfully opened a small garment factory that took work on consignment from North Italian firms, which take advantage of cheaper Southern Italian labor and weaker labor militancy to cut costs. Eight of Donato's apprentices adopted the strategy of emigration. Seven work in Northern Italy as tailors and one left for Argentina. These were Donato's earlier apprentices. His most recent eight "boys" remained in Locorotondo but had to find completely different livelihoods than those they expected to follow. There is a laundry owner, a telephone company worker, a town policeman, a municipal clerk, a bartender, a beverage distributor, and a mechanic. The two woman continue to sew pants for the few tailors who are left.

Some who trained as artisans, but who were displaced by the penetration of ready-made goods, coped by retailing factory-made versions of what they had been trained to produce. Several shoe and clothing stores in Locorotondo are owned by ex-artisans. The Smaltino cart factory, which built its last cart in 1942 and continued to repair carts until they fell into almost complete disuse in the 1960s, is now a hardware and paint store run by two Smaltino brothers. At one time the factory had a work force of fourteen men and boys and turned out as many as ninety carts a year, serving four provinces. When I talked to them, the Smaltino brothers had lovingly restored to working order a cart their father had built, and renewed its bright original colors. It sat in their back room awaiting the rumored opening of a museum of local traditional culture. The old Consoli organ factory now sells and services keyboard instruments.

Others chose to emigrate, especially during the times in the late 1950s and the early 1960s when Northern Italian industry expanded and there was a demand for labor. There was also great industrial expansion in parts of Europe beyond the Alps and many Locorotondesi from town left for Germany, Switzerland, France, Belgium, and England. A few ended up overseas in Argentina, Canada, Australia, and even South Africa. One solution, then, to the crisis was to export artisans. Some maintained their craft where they landed, and prospered. A woman from Locorotondo, for instance, became a high fashion women's seamstress in Milan, and works with top designers at the highest level of the Italian fashion industry. She married a light industrialist from the North. Others simply blended into the industrial work forces of the North and other countries, and remained. Every year, around August 15, the streets fill with cars bearing North Italian and foreign license plates. Many families and individuals who have left Locorotondo come to spend the Festival of San Rocco in their home town.

It has long been a characteristic of Italian migration, within Italy and overseas, that people leave with the intention of making their fortunes and coming back. The pull of the Italian home town is strong. Coming back to Locorotondo was sometimes the result of having prospered elsewhere, as is true of a man who learned silkscreen printing in Paris and then returned to Locorotondo. First he made plastic signs, then he specialized in making sample book covers for wallpaper companies by combining his knowledge of working with plastic with silkscreening techniques. He fills orders internationally and employs a small work force from both town and country. Other times, returning to Locorotondo was a result of failing to make it elsewhere, or of getting fed up with the foreign environment. Such failure was not necessarily the fault of the emigrant. During the 1970s the boom times that Northern Italy and other European countries had known after post-World War II reconstruction began to wane, and the great industrial cities could not hold all of the migrants and "guest-workers" Southern Italy and the rest of Southern Europe could send. In North Italy the labor unions won generous concessions and rights from management after 1968 and into the 1970s. There was an industrial slowdown followed by a move toward labor-saving technologies such as robotics, which such huge employers as the Fiat automobile company in Turin adopted quickly. Such things spelled higher unemployment in the North and fewer work opportunities. Migration and return is a part of the life-experience of many of those who came from the artisan class in Locorotondo.

Another opportunity arose in the early 1960s. During the late 1940s and the 1950s Italian government policy toward the underdeveloped south mostly revolved around agricultural development and land redistribution. These things affected Locorotondo little in comparison to certain other parts of Apulia because there was little large estate property, and grape growing, although it operated on a small scale, was generally productive, especially together with the local cooperative winery. Around 1960, Italian public policy toward southern development shifted from the idea of agricultural improvement, which had not gone far enough to promote significant economic development, to the idea of industrializing the South. The government established several heavily subsidized industrial zones and two of them, Montecatini Edison (a chemical plant) at Brindisi, and Italsider (a steel complex) at Taranto, affected towns on the Plateau of the Trulli.

Italsider employs about 150 men from Locorotondo. They commute about twenty-five miles to Taranto by daily bus from the main traffic hub of town. About three quarters of them are from town, mostly from among the artisan group. The *Italsiderini*, as they are called, earn high wages for the area, and receive good benefits. Their pay is as high as the income many white collar people receive, teachers in particular. They are unionized and the experience this provided has meant a higher degree of organizational sophistication among some of them than among the independent artisans who remain in Locorotondo's town and country work environments. Thus they founded a 110-member after-work club housed in the ground floor of a newer apartment building and there they maintain a cooperative grocery store. Unfortunately, the wholesale implantation of Italsider into the Apulian economy meant that the smoke-belching plant absorbed only a single large cohort of men, who were about forty years old during my stay in 1981-1982, and after that further hirings have been rare. The industrial development that planners hoped Italsider would spur in the area, and that would have provided more jobs, has not come about. This is largely because the government placed Italsider fully realized in a zone with little previous industrial development. Its development and later its management depended upon economic connections with the north because there were no local suppliers of machines, supplies, or raw materials. People joke that even the toilet paper in the rest rooms is imported from the north, and note that no local businesses benefit from its presence. Those few positions that open, sometimes, unfortunately, because of disablement of workers on the job, are keenly sought. Parents try, usually in vain, to activate their networks of friends and relatives to pave the way, or sometimes they even try to pay unscrupulous company functionaries to give their sons jobs.

Another adaptive strategy followed by individuals displaced from the old artisan sector and their children has been to take up new trades, most of which have to do with the servicing and repair of industrial products like automobiles, tires, appliances, electronic devices, and so on. In addition, several new trades have been added to the list necessary for constructing and maintaining dwellings. The post-World War II decades saw a boom in plumbing and in fitting houses out with electricity, thereby creating a demand for electricians and plumbers that hardly existed before. Most of the other construction trades have been monopolized by men of peasant origin, but new artisans in the town provide things like wooden and aluminum door and window frames. In fact, some metal workers and carpenters have managed to stay in business this way as the demand for locally-made tools and custom wrought iron work has lessened. Figures from the family records maintained by the municipality of Locorotondo show that men who follow so-called "old" artisan trades account for about 13.6 percent of town heads of household. Those who occupy the "new" trades account for around 11 percent. The average birth year for those in the "old" trades is 1931 (three quarters of them born between 1919 and 1943), and for those in "new" trades it is 1942 (three quarters being born between 1928 and 1955).[6] The age cohort effect with respect to trades is clear.

Finally, some working people, both men and woman, have passed into service categories. The proliferation of retail stores in Locorotondo led, of course, to a demand for people to wait on customers, and this has led to some employment for young women in particular. Other children of artisans have found employment in the public sector as policemen, secretaries, clerks, and school custodians.

Although social and economic changes at national and regional levels have affected the countryside as well as the town, it is probably the case that the changes occurring in town, which led to the gradual death of the old categories of craftsmen, have been more traumatic than in the countryside. Partially this has to do with the precariousness of the "old" artisan existence. Artisans generally owned nothing they could fall back upon; most peasants at least had a place to live and a little land that came to them when they became established at marriage. Also, the peasant category in Locorotondo had its versatility to rely upon. The mixed occupational existence that most peasant men led during their careers, sometimes working for others as field hands (or even at times in other kinds of manual labor such as road building), sometimes working for themselves doing many kinds of things on the land, may have prepared them better than the specialized training gained by artisans to absorb the shocks of social change in the post-World War II era. Often the jobless artisan's only resort was to take his skills elsewhere by migrating. As the construction trades began to get established in the countryside, the Apulian housing construction boom began to absorb postpeasant labor in a general way, bringing a prosperity to rural households that has even now evaded many families in town who have been able to adapt only precariously.

Also, the values the peasant and postpeasant population place upon hard work and family participation in it may have meant that their households were more versatile earning machines than artisan households in which, ideally, a married woman did not work outside the house. The zone has always held out more chance of work for those who were willing to be employed in the fields, and that is a tabooed choice for artisan men and women. Besides Italsider there is no large industrial employer in the zone that could absorb people from town seeking to expand family income. Some small industrial employers—the garment factories, for instance—have themselves proven to be precarious operations, and they have not always treated employees equitably with respect to pay and benefits. Of course, certain individuals of artisan origin have been able to find more prosperous existences through education or by having been lucky enough to have been around at the right time when Italsider was established. The former are part of the town's new elite.

NOTES

1. This refers to soccer leagues.
2. Pasta, beans, or soup comprise the first course in an Italian meal. Ideally the second course consists of meat and accompanying vegetables.
3. See Chapter 4, note 5.
4. Recall that Locorotondo means "round place."
5. Among them numbers Severino Gazzeloni, the flute virtuoso. Locorotondo's band graduates include two first chair flutes in major orchestras in Vienna and Venice.
6. These figures come from the family cards in Locorotondo's town hall, which I sampled randomly in 1982.

6 / Old and New Elite

Grazia was about sixty years old when I interviewed her—a daughter of the "middle bourgeoisie," as she put it. Her father was a professional man. She styled herself a rebel among young women of her generation in that she had demanded from her parents an unprecedented amount of freedom for the times before World War II. She has grown old in Locorotondo and seen considerable change in the nature of the class hierarchy and values systems. I interviewed her in her house in the historical center of town, its shelves and tables bearing the weight of several generations of immaculately kept *objets d'arts* that are family heirlooms, many of them from the nineteenth century. There were frescoed paintings on the ceiling. She spoke clearly and thoughtfully in Italian as we went through a series of questions I had prepared for her in advance about the lifestyles of Locorotondo's elite in the past.[1]

Grazia: The first great scandal was created by Signorina R., an old woman who came back from Naples via Sicily, and who rode around on a bicycle. An absurd, scandalous thing because a woman had never ridden a bicycle. But she lived elsewhere for a long time. The second . . . was me, because at sixteen I used to ride through all the streets of town and tour the countryside. And they criticized my mother for giving me permission to go out. And my sister-in-law, a great friend, . . . they wouldn't let her go out with me because she always stayed home, there was a fiancé, she couldn't do much. I would have been in the advance guard of the feminists for my town. . . .

Shoemakers . . . when the snows fell they came around to ask about sweeping the roof terraces, or hauling wood . . . because they needed a piece of bread. . . . Now it pleases me that there is no longer hopeless poverty, but I'm sorry there is too much abundance . . . because it is abundance that has led to what today's society has become. Too much money does no good. You have to know how to earn money. I repeat, my father left nothing to us, but he left a great lesson: one works to eat. If one doesn't work, one doesn't live honestly. That's where all the thefts, where all the deviance . . . where today's life comes from. You'll say that I'm very severe, that I am old fashioned. I was born that way. I haven't adapted. I live, that's all. I don't live high. Even my nieces and nephews . . . they

are good kids, but they don't live the way I do. They are a little
more casual . . . they let things go, they forget about things—the
intrinsic values of man.

Galt: Which, for you, are? Work?

Grazia: No, well . . . the whole thing . . . principally work, and, I don't
know, to have that sense of personal decorum. . . . I value rectitude
in life.

Galt: Is that characteristic of people in the better off classes?

Grazia: No! Now too much money is characteristic. Nobody knows about
sacrifices. That's why there are strikes—no one works. No one
respects anyone anymore. "What's yours is mine, and if you have
something, I have to have it." But you don't care why I have it, if I
worked for it. I don't know . . . work is my "hobby." I don't sit
around doing nothing. For me there has to be something to do each
day, otherwise I couldn't take it. But then you see people who
complain, or who are bored: "I'm tired . . . I'm sick of it." In the
evening, I find that the day has passed and I haven't been able to get
in all that I planned to do. I fill the day with work.[2]

For example, there's that freedom for young people of today
. . . all that going around without shame, without respect, without
anything . . . pretense, that's all pretense. Freedom is pretense.
. . . In the past not having freedom was exaggerated. But me, this
never weighed me down because I never accepted it. At sixteen I
said to my mother, "If you trust me and have respect for me you
have to let me go freely. Then you can rein me in if you see me
deviating from a life of rectitude, but if I have to be sacrificed in the
house, only because there's the custom of going out only accompanied by the maid or a relative . . . no, I can't accept this." There,
that's why I say I accept the liberty, or rather the independence of
the individual. You mustn't be anyone's underling. . . . I have to
respect you and you have to respect me. . . . Now I think that
because young people have everything, they have everything—they
lack for nothing—from the time they are born . . . toys . . . toys . . .
clothes . . . everything they want. There's nothing left to give them.
Trips, fun, shows . . . there is nothing. We used to dream. We
dreamed about taking a little trip to Bari; we dreamed about little
things. . . . We were happy to finally do something out of the
ordinary. Today's young people are discontented because they have
everything and they haven't anything more to work for.

THE OLD ELITE

Social class differences in town Locorotondo before the changes of the late 1950s
and early 1960s were quite marked. While no longer so blatant because considerable class mobility has occurred due to those changes, they still obviously exist. The
old social class structure of the town is fossilized in the older parts of the cemetery

Figure 6.1   Tombs of elite families in the central avenues of the cemetery.

where the ornately sculpted family vaults of the relatively wealthy landowning and professional families occupy the center and the final resting places of the many surround them. Ciccio, the ex-tailor, described how the dead loved ones of elite families rested in church on an elaborate cloth draped platform after having been borne in through the large central doors under an elaborate black cloth mantle—a privilege that cost extra. The coffins of working people lay on a carpet on the floor with a few candles and the custom was that they be brought in through the smaller doors to the side. The archpriest ended this usage in about 1940, but older people of artisan origin remember it widely and tell their descendants about it as part of the local story about social class. Those in the higher classes, or perhaps pretending to them, expected to be addressed in special ways: the title "Don," or "Donna," was to be added to their first name, and in Locorotondese dialect the personal pronoun used to address them was *"signuri"* accompanied by the third person form of the verb.[3]

The elite category of Locorotondese society resided in town and included two rough categories: those who exercised a profession, and those who aspired to live from estate income alone. Those who sold things in stores, at least if they did so lucratively, fit with the "middle bourgeoisie," but were somewhat rare—there were few stores. People considered pharmacists as professionals, even though they did not need a university education, and they played a key role among the elite because their shops were places to find a conversation. Except for a few very wealthy families, the elite houses of Locorotondo could just hope for the kind of landowner-ship that would permit living an upper class life totally from farm income, and local landowning families also earned money from professional activities, or from public administration. One of the major families of Locorotondo, for instance, ran the tax collection office for many years. Families in the professional class often owned some land, which they let out to peasants under sharecropping contracts, but not enough to gain a total income from it.

Until their decline after World War II, the old landowning families of Locor-otondo composed the highest tier of the stratificational system. These families had held that position since the early nineteenth-century when their names begin to show up in dominant positions in historical records. One family in particular was the richest in town, and owned large estates stretching from Locorotondo down to the coastal plain almost to the sea. More of its wealth came from outside Locorotondese territory than from inside. From people of all other social categories in Locorotondo I heard that this family had gained its initial wealth through associations with a famous early nineteenth-century Apulian bandit—Ciro Annichiarico, a red-haired priest turned brigand, who rode the hills and plains of the heel of Italy during the century's first two decades.[4] Although there is documentary evidence that suggests this family's association with Ciro Annichiarico in secret political machinations involving the murder of a rival for office, there is scant evidence to support the idea that this led to acquiring greater amounts of land.[5] Folk memory, in this case, is only partially correct. In reality it appears from various records that the richest families in Locorotondo gained land when the feudal lord of the area sold his estates in Locorotondo.

What is interesting, however, is the persistence of the legend and the glee with which it is told. People of other classes, especially the next lower category, the professionals, take a certain hostile pleasure in ascribing the family's wealth to illegal activities, perhaps because it is a way to express their envy symbolically. For similar reasons, individuals in the professional category also enjoyed relating stories about the ignorance of individuals in the wealthiest class, since the latter did not usually have higher education. One story involved the head of a wealthy family who, wanting to impress his guests at a gathering, greeted them at the door with what he thought was a flowery expression, "Pass over the threshold." However, he mistook the Italian word for "sole," *(sogliola)* as in the fish, for the word for "threshold" *(soglia)*. In essence, the story, apocryphal as it may be, goes that he greeted them at the door, saying: "Pass the fish!"

The landowning elites and the professionals lived in the historical center in multi-storied houses, some of them large. Several of these were ornamented with frescoes and stucco ornament and dated back several hundred years. Locorotondo was small enough that no particular urban neighborhood contained more upper class housing than any other and the richest landowners lived among the single-room dwellings of artisan neighbors. The landowners and some among the professionals also spent time during August and September in the countryside in great houses on their estates, or if there were no estates in small villas, on occasion constructed with trullo techniques. The great houses were sometimes sumptuously decorated with eighteenth-century motifs or had ornamental gardens. From such dwellings the proprietor could supervise the grain harvest and the grape picking. Country pleasures also included dinners *al fresco* and horseback riding.

The professional elites prided themselves on education, which was, of course, necessary to exercise their professions—pharmacist, doctor, lawyer, notary, teacher, surveyor. Like the working people of Locorotondo, some people in this category placed great value on work. The latter is evident in my talk with Grazia. Education was less necessary for the highest elite, and often they finished only secondary school and did not go to the university. Of course, a secondary school education was still a great deal more than the third, or more rarely, fifth grade educations that peasants and artisans received until educational reforms in the 1960s made middle school mandatory. Education for the old elite, whether at a secondary school or at a university afterward, often meant leaving Locorotondo for a period, and this contributed considerably to their more cosmopolitan outlook. At the very least it meant commuting to Martina Franca, a larger town, to attend high school, although some elite individuals I talked with finished their schooling in boarding schools in Naples, or even in the north.

The small elite social circles of Locorotondo alone did not always provide enough marriage opportunities for the young people who were part of them. Therefore marriage networks stretched outside the town's borders and landowning and professional families developed sprawling connections across the Apulian landscape to other towns. In these categories parents suggested advantageous marriage choices to young people. There were often large amounts of property at stake, and such marriages created political and business alliances for families. Parents relied upon certain self-selected elite individuals to act as go-betweens among families, often in different towns, and to initiate contacts. Grazia recalled that women from the wealthiest families held court, so to speak, in the shaded courtyards of their houses, and much of the gossip consisted of discussing what boys and what girls would be good matches for each other.

A good idea of the gulf between elites and working people in Locorotondo comes from comparing their wedding arrangements. Before World War II an upper class bride might bring 100 of each required item in a trousseau. In the countryside it was six or seven. Before the wedding it was the expectation that a middle bourgeois or landowning class fiancé give his bride-to-be *brillanti* consisting of a diamond necklace, earrings, and pin. After the wedding itself, which took place in the morning, the groom's family, if particularly well-off, provided a "lunch" (they used the English word) for many guests. This consisted of a cold buffet. In lesser households immense trays of pastries were passed about, and on both occasions they served *spumoni*, a kind of ice cream cake. My informant noted that greater households could be distinguished from lesser ones by the number of slices cut from each *spumoni*—rich households cut theirs into four slices, and poorer hosts could only afford six. Such things were the object of gossip after the celebration. But to serve *spumoni* at all was a mark of elite status.

It was important to keep family names going and to preserve heritages. Dividing land into too many pieces through marriage settlement and inheritance threatened this value. One means to preserve properties intact was known as the *maggiorasca-to*, which was the practice of passing all family lands on to the eldest son, and discouraging other children from marrying, or providing them with marriage settlements in cash only. This is a form of what anthropologists call *primogeniture*. This practice had mostly died out among the landowning families of Locorotondo by the twentieth century, but one of them practiced it into recent decades. At all levels of Locorotondese society, eldest sons are named after their father's father, second sons after their mother's father, third sons after their father's eldest brother, fourth son's after their mother's eldest brother, and so on.[6] This tends to produce an alternation of names in lines of first sons: Giuseppe di (son of) Nicola, Nicola di Giuseppe. Among the elite, whose names were broadly known, this alternation of generations, or sometimes the naming of eldest sons after their fathers so that all eldest sons bore the same name, entered the folk memory. There is a line of Don Ciccio's, for instance, remembered from the early nineteenth century and one from the mid-twentieth. In the working classes, nicknames are used more often than name, surname combinations and the pattern is less apparent, especially because many people do not even know their neighbors' surnames.

Among the professional elite land inheritance was less important, and *partible* inheritance, by which children all receive equal marriage settlements and inheritances of land, more the rule. But, families placed a strong value on preserving the profession in the family. Doctors, for instance, expected one of their grandsons to follow a medical career. For pharmacists, family succession in the profession was especially important to maintain the pharmacy, a considerable investment, in the family.

Elite townspeople placed great emphasis on form and appearance, and their use to display the nature of their status, both internally to the class and externally to other classes. Therefore they emphasized titles such as *Don* and *Donna*, already mentioned, or professional titles such as "the *Lawyer* Tizio," or "the *Notary* Caio." People also use the title *Don* to address priests. The use of titles in everyday conversation in the third person among elites, or as expectations about address by working people toward elites, constantly emphasized rank in the hierarchy. Ciccio, the tailor, recalled his schoolmaster, a position on the lower fringes of the middle bourgeoisie, demanding to be called *Don* and to be addressed with *signurì*. Others, such as doctors or landowners, whose ranks were clearer, did not need to make such demands because people deferred to them more automatically.

Two gentlemen's clubs, one for those in the professional category, and the other for those in the landowning category, both in the town center, served as rallying points for higher-class men. These corresponded to pre-fascist political parties as well as to class distinctions within the elite.[7] The professionals' club was the larger of the two, offering overstuffed armchairs, two newspaper and some magazine subscriptions, a room for playing cards, and a billiard room. Here men congregated, gossiped, kept up on news, talked politics, and played cards or billiards. The other club served similar functions but had only two rooms. People now talk about gambling among elite men of those times as a problem, and repeat stories about legendary games in which they wagered whole estates and lost them.

There were other conventions that showed rank. Those in the highest elite stayed home and others went to them. Tailors and barbers went to the houses of their high class clients to fit clothing or to give shaves. Entry into the houses of such people is part of what lent those trades prestige. The highest elite held weddings in their houses rather than in the church, and a priest in the family—or, if there were none, the locally ranking churchman—served them. There was also a get-together held at the bride's house between the engagement party and the wedding itself at which certain legal formalities concerning posting notice of the marriage were taken care of. The mayor and the archpriest attended and performed the formalities involved in the home of their elite host. Lesser couples went to the city hall, and, according to some peasant accounts, took a basket of eggs or some fruit to get the clerk to wait on them. Elite people did not carry things home. They sent someone out, or tipped a boy to carry home whatever had been purchased. A woman who was a newcomer to elite Locorotondo in the 1950s remembers being criticized for walking around the streets with a package. Middle bourgeois and landowner families had servants—at least a maid. Women, in particular, were expected to be served. The husband of the woman who carried her own package refused her permission to drive a car because a woman driving by herself was scandalous by local standards.

As in all the other classes in Locorotondo unmarried girls were carefully supervised. Grazia was a rebel because she rode a bicycle. She was unconventional and it did her reputation no good. The convention before World War II was that elite young women went out only in the company of a relative, or more often with the family maid. Of course, being accompanied on a walk or in the park by a servant was also a clear visual marker of rank and wealth. Young women of elite rank, however, had more leisure time than those from the artisan category because their days were not filled with work. They could visit each other. Few pursued education beyond elementary school, and no one expected that women would take up a profession, or even entertained the thought. There were, however a few female elementary school teachers in Locorotondo before World War II. They would have been trained through a special kind of high school, and were probably the most highly educated women in town.

THE RISE OF A NEW MIDDLE CLASS

The post-World War II era has seen a distinct leveling of social class and the rise of new roads to middle class status besides the traditional professions and landowner-ship. People have risen from artisan class origins into a new middle class, and some have, in effect, fallen from elite origins into it. As I noted in the beginning of this chapter, some individuals from the countryside also have been able to attain middle class status. New opportunities for training and employment, and new entrepreneurial activities have arisen and the economic and power base of the old landowning category has eroded, especially with respect to their lands in Locorotondo. Alongside these changes, the changes in the countryside toward an economy based upon construction trades, has considerably leveled wealth between town and country.

The landowning class fell on harder times with increasing labor costs in agriculture, falling prices (especially with respect to grapes), relatively poor land, and a complete lack of demand for the animals they used to breed on Locorotondese larger estates. Some of these families still have lands, but for reasons reported earlier, the profits that can be reaped from them have greatly shrunken. With the erosion of their landed wealth and power bases, and competition with others who have acquired wealth and power built in other ways, the old landed class has become overshadowed. A member of an old wealthy family wrote to me in answer to one of my questions to him about change in Locorotondo, that:

> The change in the dominant class became evident after the last world war. We saw a true revolutionary movement, even if bloodless. Audacious entrepreneurs, rising from nothing, have attained conspicuous economic positions; thus there has been a real overturning of the social classes.

One of the wealthiest families in town has sold part of its spacious house, and the head of another has retired to the countryside to live out his days. He declared to me that he was seriously considering planting his estate in Locorotondo in trees and allowing it to return to nature. All the children of these families have had to face the idea that they would have to attain professional degrees to make a living, since living from estate income is no longer possible. Some of them managed to do so, and find themselves homogenized, so to speak, in a new professional category composed in part of descendants of the old professionals and in part of upwardly mobile children of artisans.

Simultaneously, various new entrepreneurial opportunities have arisen in the forty-five years since the end of World War II. The penetration of ready-made products into Southern Italy killed the artisan economy, but also caused a boom in retailing. Store owners of one kind or another account for 9.5 percent of heads of family in my sampling of the family cards in the town hall. Some of these own tiny little odds-and-ends shops selling notions and household goods, or little corner tobacco shops. But lucrative businesses such as large appliance and electronics stores and fashionable clothing stores have also arisen. There is even an impressive jewelry store in a conspicuous location on the town's main avenue. There are several ready-made furniture stores and outlets that sell electrical supplies and plumbing fixtures. Growth in automobile registration in the 1960s created a demand for gas stations, garages, an auto parts store, a junk yard, and a used-car dealer. There has also been a proliferation of small groceries, of butchers, and of green grocers. In 1988 a supermarket that serves people in both town and country opened outside town along the road leading from Locorotondo to Fasano. Several excellent restaurants have also opened in Locorotondo during the past several decades; they cater to wedding parties and have enough of a reputation that people drive from as far away as Taranto or Bari to have a Sunday meal out. Café bars have sprung up all over town to supply the refreshment needs of people, as have several snack shops serving take-out roasted meat. By 1987 there was even a shop near the public park that sold local versions of hot dogs, hamburgers, and shakes. American-style fast food, for several years a feature in Italian cities, had found its way to the Plateau of the Trulli. These businesses have supplied jobs, as I noted above, but at the same time have meant good incomes and middle class status for entrepreneurs, many of them from the old working classes of the town, some from the old elite.

Employment in one aspect or another of the public sector has also ballooned. First, compulsory education through middle school, adopted in 1962, meant that many teaching positions needed to be filled, and as people realized that further education was more accessible to people outside the upper classes, more of the youth began to go on into further secondary education. This meant, of course, an expansion of teaching positions in the general region as high schools expanded and various special secondary schools such as the hotel and tourism training school in Fasano, or the day care training school in Martina Franca opened. Teachers, either employed in Locorotondo or in neighboring towns, account for 1.5 percent of heads of household, and that figure is low overall because their spouses and other married women not reflected in the data as household heads are often teachers as well.[8] Being a teacher brings in a reliable and decent income with dependable benefits and the advantage of being in the classroom only in the morning. For women the latter means that time during the day can be devoted to mothering, as well as preparing for the next day's classes, and for ambitious men, the free afternoon can be devoted to political activity. It is no accident that most of Locorotondo's political figures are teachers at one level or another. Being a teacher confers solid middle class status on people, even if the income involved is not so great as in other professional activities. Other public sector jobs that confer middle class status include various civil service office jobs in public agencies and working in the management of the cooperative winery, among others.

The expansion of this new middle class in Locorotondo, and elsewhere in Southern Italy, has brought with it a demand for new housing, and this has meant that tall condominiums, some of them containing sizeable apartments, now ring the edge of towns. It has been my impression that new middle-class housing in the area is far more pleasant and spacious than what would be available to people of the same income levels in bigger Italian cities, and that the new middle class lives quite comfortably, able to enjoy all the modern conveniences while continuing to participate in the rich social life of a small town. In 1981 the town population of Locorotondo numbered around 5,000 people, but gave the impression of being far more urban than would be a town of similar population in the United States. In the early 1980s the old historical center housed an aging population of old artisans and poorer people who could not afford to move to the new-style housing. Some descendants of the old elite families continued to live there as well.

The new middle class has also embraced the post-World War II culture of mass consumerism. Most people in it have one or more cars, a television set, a telephone, all major appliances, and stylish furniture. Many are able to take vacations elsewhere in Italy or perhaps abroad, or perhaps spend time during August on the beach in rented houses or at a resort. In short, many who are descendants of poor artisans, and who grew up under economically strained circumstances—many children in small dwellings—now live lives that can be considered as comfortable as those lived by the elites as recently as the 1950s. As in the United States, rising prices have, however, caused many to follow the adaptive strategy of putting both husband and wife to work, and, especially among teachers, the dual income family is common.

CHANGING VALUES AND IDEAS

The town boasts a greater variety of people, and, through the elite and through outsiders such as national police officers *(carabinieri)* stationed there, it has been the main point of contact with the world outside Locorotondo. This means that customs and behavior have tended to change there more radically than in the countryside. Consider also that the crisis for artisans meant emigration experiences for more of them than for peasants. This too has brought new ideas and experiences to town more than to the countryside. For instance, some magical beliefs I described for the peasant population earlier have disappeared in town, but remain in the rural zones, at least in the heads of older people. One quite elderly woman from town found my description of the living belief in the *ajure* from rural zones an amusing thing she barely remembered from her childhood. However, other magical beliefs, in the evil eye for instance, are widespread in both urban and rural Southern Italy in one form or another, and remain strong in the town as well as the country of Locorotondo.

Significant changes have come about in the town of Locorotondo with respect to the behavior of young people. In 1962 Italy extended compulsory education through middle school, and rising aspirations for middle-class careers among town people have meant that many parents see the education of children through high school and university as desirable, if not necessary. Few young people go into apprenticeships at the early ages their parents did, although many go to work after they have completed middle school. In general young people have more time on their hands than did their parents. In addition, like young people the world over, they are greatly influenced by youth fads and fashions, especially international rock music culture, that emphasize decision making autonomy from parents and other authorities while increasing demands on family budgets to provide fashionable clothing and other requisites of adolescent life. Over the radio the youth of Locorotondo hear many of the same songs the youth of an American city hear, and these are played by ebullient disk jockeys who insert American English words and phrases into their patter. Enough of them take English in middle school that they can even make out some of the lyrics they hear. Similarly, affluent Locorotondese teens buy clothing at a Benetton store in Martina Franca essentially equal to the branch of this enterprising Italian company in the reader's local mall or downtown.

In town these processes have gone much further than in the countryside where values about hard work, and wanting to earn some money to put away to start a family, send most young people into a full work life just after graduating from middle school. There are fewer pressures to attain further education. Instead, town children of people socialized in the artisan milieu now copy the leisurely behavior that was more typical of the elite in the past. In late afternoon they descend upon the center of town to take part in the evening *passeggiata*, or stroll, something that in the past only those who did not need to work constantly for a living could permit themselves. The main street of Locorotondo fills with men sitting on benches, strolling together up and down the sidewalks, lolling about the doors of social clubs, and buying one another coffees and aperitifs in café bars. The *Villa Communale*, or municipal park, swells with adolescent boys and girls who walk, usually in same-sex groups, round and round its outer perimeter, stopping occasionally to joke and gossip, or to admire the magnificent view that stretches out over the valley below to Martina Franca in the distance. The fact that many bureaucratic jobs have only morning hours, and schools only meet in the morning, allows these leisure hours for those who can enjoy them. Parents with middle class aspirations for their children rarely require them to work after school, and they are released to the social life of the park and town streets where young people find it very important to be seen.

The scene is animated and full of intense adolescent drama spiced with flirting, gossip, and envy. Some teenagers of our acquaintance, who for peculiar biographical reasons considered themselves town girls exiled in the countryside, enviously described the park scene as full of *"movimento."* Those boys who have managed to buy cars or motor scooters buzz about the townscape, stopping at the park entrance to talk to and perhaps impress groups of girls circling the path. Some of these girls even get in or climb aboard to cruise about. In short, the old days of only a few

Figure 6.2   The public garden crowded with people after Sunday Mass.

decades ago, when mere glances between young men and young women could be an intense experience because of their sheltering from one another, are gone. It was not unusual in 1982 to see town couples nuzzling each other in public, and Donato, the elderly tailor, exclaimed to me with great exasperation that they sometimes did so right in front of his shop.

Another factor in the liberation of the town youth from the highly controlled life led in the past has been education, both in the sense that the curriculum itself has brought a more cosmopolitan view of the world to Locorotondo, but also in the sense that being in school, and therefore away from home, has become extended into the adolescent years when most people in earlier generations finished school with the fifth grade and then faced going to work under tightly controlled circumstances. For those who attend more than middle school, high school means daily travel to a neighboring town on a bus or a train. This provides abundant opportunities to mingle with the opposite sex with no supervision and to meet people from other towns. Such experiences began with a few pioneers from town during the 1960s who attended the scientific or classic high schools in Martina Franca, and have expanded significantly as more specialized trade schools have opened and as more have gone on for further education.

In short, things have changed greatly and people have broader sets of expectations about their life's careers both in the strict sense of vocation and in the broader sense of choices about marriage partners and about lifestyles. The greater variety of choice may threaten older people fully socialized in values that have become challenged by economic change and by competition with powerful national, and even international, ways of thinking and symbolism particularly about consumerism. Some of this threat is visible in what Grazia, the daughter of the old middle-bourgeoisie, says. Greater choice has also meant that finding a niche in local society can be difficult, especially for the educated. Throughout the 1970s there were simply not enough slots in the bureaucracy, in school teaching, or in the professions, for everyone who chose those paths in Southern Italy, much less in Locorotondo. Staying in Locorotondo could mean frustrating unemployment even with a university degree and, in turn, long-term dependency on parents. Getting a job was something of a struggle and people adopted strategies that involved attempting to manipulate the system to their personal advantage. The next chapter addresses the nature of how people perceive and deal with such systems.

NOTES

1. Interviewing the elite in Locorotondo was something of a challenge because they set up barriers. There are stereotypes about the diffidence of peasants in Southern Italy, and they have a basis in truth—peasants, who have long been exploited and swindled by the more literate, have some reason to suspect the motives of educated people who approach them. However, the strongest cases of diffidence that I encountered in the field occurred when I tried to approach the old landowning and professional elite. This may have been beause my residence in a hamlet and my field assistant smacked of the countryside to them. Grazia was something of an exception in her openness, but even she wanted to see a list of written questions before consenting to an interview.

2. Grazia passes a great deal of time helping the sick and elderly of all classes through a church organization.

3. This is like Spanish *Usted,* or standard Italian *Lei,* which have similar origins, but have evolved into polite forms of the "you" pronoun to be used with people who are unfamiliar or with whom there is a strong status difference.

4. The interested reader might want to consult the colorful account of Sir Richard Church's successful defeat of this bandit under the hire of the Neapolitan crown. It was written by his daughter on the basis of General Church's diaries and gives the flavor of the times, even if every historical detail is not accurate (Church, 1895).

5. The evidence consists of eyewitness accounts of meetings between the family head and Ciro Annichiarico in 1816. I found these in the voluminous records of the murder trial in the National Archives in Bari (*Sacra Regia Udienza, Antichi Tribunali, Processi Penali,* folder 13). Tax records from the time indicate no sudden acquisition of land that can be ascribed to anything but normal purchase. There is, however, evidence from the trial documents that this family was involved in contraband. This was not uncommon during those turbulent times, and many families rose in wealth out of such activities.

6. This was also the pattern for naming feamle children.

7. The early decades of the twentieth century knew heated and sometimes violent political competition between two local parties, the Senussi and the Beduini, named after north African tribes. The Senussi were affiliated with the Italian Liberal Party and composed mostly of professionals. They dominated municipal government. The other party was more conservative and composed mostly of landowners. The one-party politics of fascism ended political competition between them, but factional sentiments lived on, as they seemingly always have in Locorontondo.

8. Spouse's occupation is not indicated in the data source—the town family cards—I consulted.

7 / Ordinary People, Paperwork, and Authority

So far I have described society in Locorotondo's countryside and in the town, and said something about the relationships between them. However, I have related little about how Locorotondo's populations connect to the world outside the town, except to note that many individuals find employment in other towns and cities, and that some have emigrated and returned. Another way people connect to other places, especially central places for Italian society, is through paperwork—i.e., through the bureaucracies they must encounter regularly. In Locorotondo people relate to bureaucracies and other centers of power and authority in ways that are reasonably typical in Southern Italy. To understand questions of how ordinary people deal both with the problems arising from bureaucratic authority, and problems that might be solved through bureaucratic authority, it is necessary to look at how people perceive the world of paperwork to operate and grasp how they develop strategies about that world. It is also important to understand the local political ramifications of such perceptions and relationships. By this I mean that it is crucial to understand how they relate to the local struggle to gain and maintain power, and how dependencies between less and more powerful people develop through those struggles.

A CONVERSATION WITH MARIO

As in other chapters, it is good to start with the words of someone I interviewed and use them to develop and illuminate principal themes. Mario is an educated man, engaged in local leftist politics, who shares in certain town prejudices about country people.

Galt: Whose word goes in Locorotondo?
Mario: I believe that among the people of Locorotondo there is a subordinate attitude in the face of established power. It's a very obvious attitude. And also it's based on ancient tradition—an attitude that goes back to extremely remote times. When the citizen of Locorotondo needs to have even an elementary right satisfied, he must always turn to "the one with power."[1] Even when requesting a birth certificate—a simple right every citizen has—he is forced to turn to certain people, seen, however, not as municipal employees serving the community, but as expressions—as branches—of power. Therefore, for an aspect of a

citizen's life, such as getting a building permit, he must first turn to an engineer or a surveyor to draw up the plans. Often, even the surveyor or the engineer is seen as a branch of the power structure. The issuance of the permit is not considered as a right, but, here too, as a gracious favor granted by a power structure bending over from on high toward the lowly. I ask for something I have a right to get because the law guarantees me these rights, but I have to ask it of someone who has the power to decide whether to give it to me or not.

Whose word goes? . . . That is a matter of [people] being able to exert leverage using a natural and historical atavistic feeling of subjection held by a large part of the population, and at the same time satisfying [their] individual needs by successfully distributing favors and sometimes [by making] threats. I give you something on the condition that you behave in a certain way. That is, at an opportune moment I can remind you of the favor that I have done for you, and I can also take it back. This, therefore, creates a situation of permanent subjugation of citizens with respect to official power. . . . And this situation is accepted by the majority of the population as a natural fact. There are those whose word goes, and to avoid hassles and to live tranquilly it becomes necessary to obey certain rules.

Galt: Is this feeling more widespread among those from the country, or among those from town? Is there a difference in this attitude?

Mario: I think this attitude is more widespread among the country people, and probably because of their having lived far from the center—therefore far from the centers of decision making—leads to less control over these same decision-making centers. And then the type of scattered settlement that exists here in Locorotondo, because of which there lack . . . until a short while ago there lacked, social relations and therefore an exchange of ideas among various citizens . . . Scattered settlement meant intellectual and cultural isolation and therefore accentuated this phenomenon of subjugation even more.

Galt: But is there more, let's say, cleverness among town people, that is, the artisan group, toward the centers of power? I know a little about how the Christian Democrats, the power center, utilized certain lists like a kind of weapon to make people in the countryside obey. Is there an analogous thing for the artisan class in town?[2]

Mario: Let's say that the artisan needs to count on official authority less because the type of work he does makes him self-sufficient in a certain way. But, look, even here there are almost imperceptible, invisible, channels, let's say, through which Christian Democratic power succeeds in consolidating itself. A more commonplace example? Here there are traffic signals. There are traffic signals just as in all civilized countries, but, look, they don't get respected. It might seem to be a matter of custom. But I think that even through this there has developed a certain way of doing politics. That is, I don't insist upon—"I" as a traffic cop, or as a municipal administrator—I don't insist upon your respecting these traffic signals as I should. In short, I let you live, I let you alone, I let you do as you please. And out of this comes, there comes this sort of laxity, this letting people do what they please according to their whims; there comes out of this a type of [political] consent that gets captured from people and is based exactly on peoples' attitude about minding their own business, about being individualists by nature. Laws, norms, when they oblige both those with power and those who endure it, become great things. But rules, when they are things that I control and that I can slacken according to my pleasure . . . this too is a way of binding people [to power], let's say, of capturing their consent.

Galt: Are you talking about manipulation of laws?
Mario: Yes, that is, giving people the impression that beyond the notable people who are here, beyond their desires, laws count for little and therefore it happens that, even for the most trivial need . . . people are so strongly inculcated with this principle that, instead of residing in the certainty of law, here power resides in the hands of those who manage community things, right here and right now. That's why people need to keep on behaving in a certain way to get certain rights.

LOCAL ADMINISTRATIVE AND POLITICAL INSTITUTIONS

Before elaborating on the themes my interview with Mario introduces, it is important to present at least a sketch of administrative and political institutions as they exist in a municipality the size of Locorotondo. The governing bodies of an Italian commune, or municipality, are in many ways parallel to the structures found in the Italian national government, which operates by parliamentary democracy. Leaders at both levels are elected indirectly. Their rise to office is a matter of political struggle carried out among the members of various parties contending for power within legislative bodies. At the national level, the president, otherwise a figurehead, forms the government, which in Italy (as in England) means the prime minister and his ministers. He does this based on a likely vote of confidence by parliament. At the municipal level the executive body, the *giunta*, is formed from among the parties in control of the *consiglio communale*, or municipal council, and consists of the mayor and a group of assessors, each charged with a specific department of local government. The communal council is responsible among other things, for passing a budget, for legislating ordinances that fall within its purview, and for deliberating upon zoning restrictions (or for granting variances from them). A town administration, just as the Italian national government, can go into crisis and fall if the often shaky consensus among party factions and parties falls apart. If the municipal council cannot reach a consensus about important issues like forming the *giunta* or defining the town budget, provincial authorities take over the operation of the town's administration until new elections can be held, theoretically within a three-month period. Thus municipal politics in Italy contains much deal making and jockeying for position among local politicians. The struggle for power takes place both between and within parties. Large parties such as the Christian Democrats have internal factions, and the splits between them can be as severe as the splits between differing parties. This means that there is considerable competition for votes among politicians.

Besides the elected communal councilors, a municipality has various civil service employees, headed by the Communal Secretary, the mayor's technical advisor, who work in the town hall and who take care of day to day business such as keeping records about the population, seeing to matters of public works, and issuing licenses and certificates. Other significant local public institutions include the elementary and middle schools (for Locorotondesi further secondary education must be sought in neighboring towns), and the hospital. These are the largest public sector employers in town. Police authority in a town Locorotondo's size is divided between the *Vigili Urbani,* the local police, whose function it is to enforce local ordinances and deal with traffic within communal boundaries, and the *Carabinieri,* or state police, who investigate criminal activities, and who are organized in a more military fashion. The *Polizia Stradale,* or highway police, take care of the roads between towns, and the *Guardia della Finanza,* or finance guards, investigate tax evasion and other fiscal crimes, but neither force has a headquarters in Locorotondo. The national police forces are generally composed of men who are not of local origin so that they are less subject to local pressures; the *Vigili Urbani* are often local people.

Post-World War II Italy is well-known for its proliferation of political parties covering a broad spectrum from left to right. While there are many parties, in most of Italy only a couple of them prevail at the local level, and in most of Southern Italy, the Christian Democratic Party (hereafter DC for *Democrazia Cristiana*) has dominated local and regional politics since shortly after World War II. In the rest of Italy, both at national and local levels, the parties of the left, the Italian Communist Party and the Italian Socialist Party, have provided considerable political competition for the DC, particularly during the 1970s and 1980s. In Locorotondo, however, the Southern pattern holds strongly, and one faction or another of the DC has dominated local politics for several decades with only one deviation. All other parties represented in the municipal council stand out of power and must either cooperate with or oppose (as the case may be, issue by issue) the DC. Local communists are usually in opposition and their members enjoy declaring that the Christian Democrats are "neither Christian nor democratic!" Parties other than the DC gained small electoral bases from various sources. For instance, the Liberal Party (in Italy, slightly to the right of center) has a doctor at its head, and being of country origin, he could count upon reaping some rural votes for his party list. He was popular in his own zone of the countryside because he could be counted upon to make house calls, even at night. The leftist parties had small memberships of ideological true believers, as did the far-right-wing Italian Social Movement, heir to Mussolini's fascist party. The Communist party has greater visibility in the community than the other small parties, however, because it maintains a party office on the main street of the town where members, most of them artisans, hang around playing cards and engaging in discussions, and because of its affiliation with the Labor Hall (see below).

Although the Christian Democratic party dominates the local electoral scene, the range of party choices in Locorotondo provides politically oriented social groups for individuals of widely diverging ideological preferences from far right to far left. In comparison to the political outlets available in a rural American town of comparable size, the Locorotondese political spectrum is quite broad and encompassing. For instance, leftists—members of the Communist and Socialist Parties and smaller leftist groups—can participate in a broader political scene that for awhile included the publication in nearby Martina Franca, of a trullo region newspaper called *Town and Country (Città e Campagna)*, which published exposés, opinion pieces, and cultural articles. Parties have offices that are centers for socializing, and Locorotondo even boasts a small cooperative bookstore that carries left-leaning publications, and serves as a focus for political and social companionship. Even if consistently outgunned by the Christian Democrats, Locorotondo's left-leaning citizens can feel solidarity in their own political world, much like that described by David Kertzer in his study of Communist-dominated Bologna, although it stretched over a larger territory.[3]

In a commune the size of Locorotondo, local elections, which, barring a crisis, are held every four years, and work by the party list system with preferential votes. Instead of voting for individual candidates running as members of parties, voters elect a list of candidates running under the auspices of a given party. Each party gains council seats by a formula based upon election totals. In addition, voters have the option to cast up to four preferential votes for individuals whose names or list numbers must be written in. They also may cross candidates off the list, and can therefore vote against an individual without having to vote for another, but people rarely exercise this option. In a sense, the contest combines the functions served by both the primary and general election in the United States into one event; it is simultaneously a competition between parties and between individuals within parties. However, the system of preferential voting partially disenfranchises illiterate voters, who vote for parties (the party symbols are pictured on the ballots), but may be put off by the necessity to write in candidates. Consequently, and perhaps out of apathy as well, many voters vote only for a party list, not choosing to cast preferential votes. The candidate vote is therefore smaller than the total number of voters, and in a small town this means that a politician who can mobilize even relatively small numbers of preferential votes among friends, relatives, and people who owe him favors, can do much toward insuring a seat on the municipal council. The preferential vote becomes an important way to repay favors done by politicians. Numbers of preferential votes decide which candidates occupy the seats won by the parties running lists in the election. Usually the person winning the most votes on the winning party list, almost always the DC in Locorotondo, assumes the position of mayor, which is generally the most significant power position in town. Sometimes, however, there is maneuvering and compromise among factions that may result in the seating of a runner up in the mayoral chair.

The national labor organizations, the CISL (Italian Confederation of Worker

Unions), the CGIL (General Italian Confederation of Labor), are related to the political parties and also maintain offices in town.[4] In Locorotondo these groups do little labor organizing in the conventional sense of the term; they are not much concerned with organized struggles for better pay and working conditions. Partially this is because there are no large-scale employers in the immediate vicinity, and the industrial workers at Italsider in Taranto are organized elsewhere. Rather, the *patronati*, as they are called, serve as organized go-between institutions that help people cope with bureaucratic problems of various kinds—filling out forms, writing letters, and understanding rules and regulations. They also handle occasional individual labor grievances. In a sense they dole out organized patronage— therefore the name *patronato*. Many of these bureaucratic matters have to do with the complexities of the Italian system of social security, which includes medical insurance, disability pensions, old age pensions, and unemployment insurance, among other things. Many Locorotondesi of the older generations are ill-equipped to deal with such matters by themselves because of inadequate literacy, and rely upon functionaries at the union offices to help them.

The two major union offices and their bureaucrats are, as noted above, affiliated with political parties. The CISL is closely associated with the DC, and the CGIL with the leftist parties, especially the PCI (Italian Communist Party).[5] Thus the former is one center of Christian Democratic power in Locorotondo and the center of one of the party's more powerful factions. The local head of CISL has been mayor and enjoys the preferential votes of many who belong to that union and who use its services. Although the Communist and Socialist parties were relatively weak in terms of votes in Locorotondo during my stay and, in fact, during most of the post-World War II era the office of the CGIL, or the Labor Hall (*Camera di Lavoro*), was an important center for people who needed help with their affairs. This was especially true because the man who ran the office was friendly and genuinely interested in helping people out. (One need not be a member of the CGIL, or be a professed leftist, to turn to the Labor Hall.) He was a retired country postman and had gained the confidence of many in rural Locorotondo by helping them out as he made his rounds. Postmen have often been significant figures in the countryside for this reason; they often did more than just deliver the mail.[6] He and everyone else realized that although the Labor Hall often made a difference for people in their daily struggles with the complexities of bureaucracy, such help did little to recruit members or votes for the leftist parties.

SCHOOLING AND CIVIL SERVICE EXAMINATIONS

All Locorotondesi face school, and many of them face the necessity to take civil service examinations (*concorsi*) after graduation. Since the 1960s, eight years of education through Middle School (*Scuola Media*) have been compulsory. Many stop after eight years, especially in the countryside, but more and more parents are sending their children on to secondary school, either to academically-oriented programs, or into trade schools. Unless a student wishes to pursue a specialization in agriculture, especially viticulture (growing grapes) and oenology (wine making), available at the local Agricultural Institute, further schooling means daily travel to another town where an appropriate school offers courses. In the preceding chapter I noted how this had changed the lives of many young people in Locorotondo. The proliferation of schools in the area over the post-1960s era has meant job opportunities for teachers and for supporting staff, although there is stiff competition for posts.

Competition for posts in the public sector beyond the level of the municipality depends in great part upon how a person scores on civil service examinations, and for many other kinds of jobs, in business and elsewhere, upon the "maturity" exam, taken as a student finishes secondary education. To get a middle-school teaching job, for instance, a person must complete a university education and then compete by examination for available jobs. Such examinations cover general knowledge. To transfer to another level within the educational system (which is national, not local) further examinations must be faced. A person often faces competitive examinations throughout his or her adult life, as new opportunities present themselves.

PERSONALISM

There is a strong attitude found in Southern Italy that is sometimes called "personalism." By this term I mean that individuals often tend to perceive their own interests as of intense importance, as opposed to those of the collective, and often they think of institutions associated with the collectivity—political and bureaucratic institutions such as those just described—as operating unfairly against personal and local interests. Such attitudes exist, I am sure, in most societies, but in Southern Italy personalism seems more openly expressed than, say, among North Americans. (I should note that there are also ideological pockets in Southern Italy in which there are strong expressions about the desirability of maximizing collective good: voices within the church and the Communist Party are two examples.) In some places in Southern Italy the personalistic view has become symbolically elaborated and deeply embedded in cultural perceptions to the point of becoming a strong enough value to receive a label in local ways of speaking. This is the case in Sicily, where the term *omertà* denotes the attitude by which local interests *should* supersede broader ones and individuals discourage one another from appealing to outside authority under any circumstances. This attitude has been important to the mafia phenomenon on that island. The attitude of personalism is not as strongly expressed in Locorotondo as in Sicily, but it certainly exists among many people and strongly influences the strategies individuals and families use in their dealings with the structures of authority described in the last section.

For example, when someone buys a used car in Italy the legal procedure is to make out transfer of ownership papers (the *passaggio*), get insurance, and pay the annual tax if it is due. The transfer of ownership implies a hefty fee—about 100,000 lire (or $85 when fieldwork was completed in the early 1980s). The paperwork for the transfer can take many weeks and people find the fee high, especially when the cost of a small used car might be about 500,000 lire. So what people do is go to a notary and make out a contract that records the sale of the car (for much less than the actual sale to avoid sales taxes) so that no accusation of theft can be made. With this document it is possible, with a few well-chosen misrepresentations to the clerk at the agency, to buy insurance. If the highway police catch the car's new owner, the fine for not having done the transfer is much lower than the transfer fee, so people feel it is worth the risk of being apprehended. In fact, some car sellers may refuse to go through with the transaction if the buyer insists upon doing things according to the law because they have not made a legal transfer from yet another owner and would face that trouble and expense. If caught, the worst that can happen is that the car's registration papers may be impounded until a proper transfer is completed. Sometimes it is possible to convince the police that the car was rented from the previous owner, which is the strategy one must adopt anyway to pay the annual tax fee at the post office. People do not go without insurance because there is a penalty of six months in jail and the risk is much too great in case of an accident. Also, going without paying the annual tax (in 1981 about 11,000 lire on a small car) is not worth it because the fine for not doing so is higher than the tax. These are normal strategies for getting a used car, and as I asked about them I was assured of this by many people, including an off-duty highway policeman. They exemplify personalism—local and personal needs are more important than nationally mandated laws.

THE OFFICIAL SYSTEM AND THE REAL SYSTEM

I proposed some time ago, based on a study on the Sicilian island of Pantelleria, that people conceive of parallel channels for achieving goals when dealing with bureaucracies (Galt, 1974). One perceived channel, which I have called "the official system," is written and codified in the law; it consists of the regular bureaucratic ways for doing things. It is the paperwork system, and many people perceive it as poorly organized at best—inconvenient, perhaps even corrupt, and something a person must either skirt or know how to manipulate through personalistic strategies to achieve desired goals. They talk of the official system as stemming from processes of decision making that are alien and unresponsive to local and personal needs.

On the other hand, personalistic values, actions, and social ties comprise the "real system" of strategies by which individuals try to evade the inconveniences and discomforts, and perhaps the crises, produced for them by the official system. Not only does the real system provide these advantages, but people see it as humanizing something otherwise considered as cold and inflexible. Attempting to operate with real system strategies, although not always successful, provides, I think, a certain satisfaction for many people because it becomes an expression of individuality—of personal power. This is not a cultural system in which blind following of authority is a value—the person who does so is a fool. The person who knows how to skirt authority is clever (*furbo*) and gains respect from that.

It is extremely important to note that these parallel systems are *perceptions* upon which people feel compelled to operate. Not all Southern Italian bureaucracies are necessarily corrupt or inefficient, and real system strategies—invoking the aid of patrons, for instance—do not always work. Often the risks are too great, as they would be in the car buying example when it comes to going without automobile insurance. The real system works primarily through two related strategies: (1) the patron client relationship, and (2) skirting official regulations in hopes of not being caught, or of getting off lightly if caught.

PATRON-CLIENT RELATIONS

Patron-client relations are a special form of social exchange relationship and an important structure in which personalistic values get played out. Exchange is very much at the heart of relationships between individuals outside the sphere of the family in Locorotondo.[7] Even close and warm friendships revolve around the idea that friends give each other things and exchange favors. In rural neighborhoods people often quote the proverb: "As the basket comes and goes; friendships are maintained." This proverb is a literal description of behavior because neighbors in good standing with one another often make small presents consisting of things like fruit, or freshly baked almond cookies, or perhaps some newly-made cheese, to each other. Figuratively, the proverb suggests that good relationships are based upon regular exchange. Such exchange, as several classic social theorists have pointed out, must be lagged over time to tie people together.[8] If the Giovanni Palmisano family sends a child next door to the Giuseppe Cardone family with some nice ripe figs, Giuseppe's wife Graziella would not immediately send a gift back. Rather, at some time in the future she would reciprocate with a small favor or a small gift. The lag creates on-going obligations between people. As people become closer to each other in Locorotondo, as in other places I have experienced in Southern Italy, the obligation of immediate reciprocation lessens. In Locorotondo a person who has been done a favor by someone who is merely an acquaintance, not a friend or neighbor, will ask politely what can be done to "take away the obligation." The equally polite response is to say that nothing needs to be done. This does not mean that there is no obligation; it means that the person who has done the favor is open to a continuing relationship and that turn-about is expectable someday. However, basing neighborly and friendly relationships in exchange does not rule out warmth. Families and individuals involved in such relationships often associate and have fun together informally. (It is sometimes hard for some North Americans to grasp the idea that Southern Italian relationships outside the family are based upon exchange, because their ideology of friendship stresses mutual affection between friends, before thinking about their usefulness.)

The idea of exchange also strongly colors ties between people who are not warm friends or neighbors, but who mainly stand to one another in complex interdependencies concerning power, in other words, in patron-client relationships. In Locorotondo, as in other parts of Southern Italy, such relations are called *amicizia*, which an Italian/English dictionary would define as "friendship," but that in local Italian, and in dialect, means both the warmer kind of friendship, and the relationship between patrons and clients. Someone referring to "a friend of mine" (*un mio amico*), could either be talking about an equal who he or she liked and saw or someone to whom he or she would turn if in need of help in accomplishing something complicated, usually concerning a bureaucracy. (The English idiom, "having friends in high places," conveys something similar.) It would be extremely important to pay attention to the context of the conversation.

Patron-client relationships bind together people who are unequal with respect to the control of important resources, especially personal connections to external centers of power. Often the inequality between those involved in such a relationship stems from social class differences and is more or less permanent. But frequently because of a factor such as employment in a particular office, or knowing a particular person, one person may have access to resources to which another does not. In such cases the inequality is not so much social as a matter of particular circumstances. An ambitious individual having such entrée may provide himself with a foundation for creating obligations with others who need contacts. In present-day Locorotondo patrons and clients are probably more often near social equals than they were in the past because of the flattening of the system of social stratification that has taken place in the last several decades (see Chapter 5), and because far more people are literate than were in the not-so-distant past. (Where there is widespread illiteracy, or only partial literacy, those who can handle words and paper find themselves in a potentially powerful situation.) Some who do favors may do so out of a sense of good will, others may do them with an eye toward calling in the implicit obligations created for their own purposes later. This, of course, depends upon individual levels of ambition with respect to power, particularly political power.

Patrons do their clients favors that have to do with bureaucracies and paperwork. Such favors revolve around the idea of *racommandazione*, literally "recommendation." The meaning of this term goes beyond the sense of "letter of recommendation" Americans might associate with it. If in Italian I say "I recommend you to Tizio," it means that I *entrust* you to Tizio, who will see after your needs. To cite a small but common example, occasionally my family and I went out to eat in one of Locorotondo's restaurants where we ran into local middle-class acquaintances. They would invariably admonish the waiter, or the proprietor, by saying that they knew us and that we should be treated well. Such admonitions always ended with the phrase "*vi raccommando!*" This exchange implies the following: "These are my friends, and I am entrusting them to you so that you will serve them well." The theme of personalism is expressed well in this example because the polite phrase moves the diner away from the impersonal status of off-the-street restaurant patron into the personalistic status of having been entrusted to the restaurant's staff by people to whom the restaurateur might have to answer if the service or food turns out to be bad. Everyone involved feels special: the diners because they are no longer just part of a herd; the local patron, who has the gratitude of the diners; and the restaurateur, who has the special opportunity to please and perhaps capture a new regular customer, and who may feel flattered because the local patron trusts the restaurant's quality enough to say something. Sets of mutual obligations, even if of a minor sort, have been activated. This is a miniature patron-client relationship. Of course, most things that patrons do for clients are more important than trying to assure a good meal in a restaurant, but the example serves to show how pervasive patron-client behavior is.

People appeal to potential patrons to help them get jobs, to help their children get higher scores on examinations, to help with social security paperwork, to deal with university bureaucracies, and to get licenses and permits, among other things. People express a strong sense that without a personalizing tie to someone with leverage, someone who can manipulate officialdom, a person's needs will be overlooked. People operate in the "real system" to manipulate the "official system" so as to safeguard their interests. People recognize that paperwork is also important and attempt to get things filled out and filed correctly, but they "hedge their bets" with appeals to real or potential patrons. I think they do this to have a sense of doing something *personal* about situations that are often unpredictable. For instance, on civil service exams there is a sense that a person both needs to do well and have some help from someone.

Patron-client strategies cannot always work, however. Sometimes, for instance, someone thought of as having control over a particular resource will be overwhelmed with simultaneous requests for help by potential clients. Also, those making such requests may have inflated expectations about the kind of help a would-be patron might be able or willing to provide. I recall one summer weekend with Martino, a teacher friend who was involved at the time in giving the maturity examination to graduating high school students in a large city nearby. The grade received on this exam—a final examination for a person's high school education— can be very important in seeking jobs later, and the exam is a source of worry for both students and parents. As I spent time with my friend, person after person approached him on the street, or at home by telephone, asking his help for a relative, or a relative of a friend, who would be taking the examination in the city where he was to give and grade it. Martino, his wife, and I had the impression that parents in the city had used their networks of friends to find out who the examiners were, and then racked their brains to think of acquaintances or relatives in Locorotondo and other towns from which examiners come who might be able to approach them. Martino is a person of high ideals and a strong believer in education, and it is very unlikely that he would ever favor one student over another. To deflect requests for patronage he would ask those who approached him whether their student had studied hard, and assured them that if this were so everything would go well. Martino and his wife joked all weekend that it was too bad he did not have political ambitions because he could probably garner many local preferential votes by making promises. It was obvious to the three of us, however, that even if he had made such promises, a knotty dilemma would have arisen. Too many people talked to him about their student friends and relatives. It would have been impossible to do favors for them all and get away with it. Other individuals involved in a similar situation, and more interested in playing power games, might have reassured at least some of these supplicants with vague promises.

In fact, others who occupy strategic bureaucratic positions may play the patron role to the hilt. Some use the local image of the bureaucracy as inadequate to create a need for their intercession. A simple way to do this is for the bureaucrat to adopt an aloof stance toward people coming in for his or her services. For instance, I can recall standing at the counter alone in a bureaucratic office for a long time attempting to get the attention of the head of the office, who when he finally

*Figure 7.1   "Personalism" in traffic. A downtown Bari street corner; most of the
cars shown are parked.*

deigned to turn his attention my way, barked at me, I thought rudely, to remove my
notebook from his counter. I often saw this functionary strolling around the *piazza*
during working hours, or hanging around in the café bars. His behavior made it
clear to me, and to others I talked to, that to enjoy the services he was supposed to
provide the citizenry, a personalistic connection, perhaps even a small gift was
necessary. Many, especially older people from the countryside, still come to town
to conduct business armed with small gifts of eggs or fruit, or perhaps some wine, to
bestow upon functionaries, although leveling of social class differences means that
more people than in the past come equipped, instead, with a sense of their rights.

SIDESTEPPING OFFICIAL REGULATIONS

Mario's discussion of roadway rules provides a good example of another way the
real system and official system are interrelated. Consider parking, for instance. The
North American or North European visitor to Southern Italy is struck immediately
by the fact that people park cars with great creativity, wheels drawn on to the
sidewalk, around corners, or even on the wrong side of the street, facing against
traffic. All these individual solutions to the parking problem are illegal. There is,
however, a personalistic sense in Locorotondo, and in other Southern Italian places,

that such official system rules need not apply locally if no great harm is done in violating them. Indeed, they are rarely enforced, opening the possibility of creative individual solutions to a parking problem that is enormous in big cities, and can be annoying even in a smaller town like Locorotondo. Of course, the solution proves irksome to pedestrians who must negotiate their way down sidewalks through the narrow spaces left between buildings and cars, and who in a city like Bari face a challenge at each intersection because the spaces between parked car bumpers are so narrow that finding a place to step off the sidewalk and cross the street takes a few moments searching.

In Locorotondo a driver can often sidestep certain traffic laws without much fear of legal action. However, as Mario notes for traffic signals, the eye that traffic policemen close to violations might open. In a small town like Locorotondo such rules may not be enforced but *could be* selectively. As Mario claims, this gives an administration power because the official system of laws could be invoked any time and individuals could be caused trouble selectively. In essence, this is a price that people pay for flexibility in solving individual problems—they at least fear that displeasing law enforcers and the administration behind them could create difficulties. Mario talks of looseness in law enforcement, and its potential selective application, as a way of creating a political consensus for the power structure at the municipal level.

Other, perhaps more significant areas where people say personalistic infractions frequently exist include building codes and zoning laws, and the social security system. Zoning laws and building codes are relatively new to this area of Italy, the former mandated for each municipality by a 1968 law. This directive created a chaotic political struggle in Locorotondo and similar towns. It resulted in a zoning law seen by the rural population as far too restrictive of their rights to build housing for their marrying children on parentally owned land. The upshot was that many families have constructed housing that is too large for the land area it is located upon, using various ruses to disguise dwelling space as agricultural work space when building inspectors came around. There can be greater square footage occupied by work space than by living space. Everyone in Locorotondo is well aware of this, and if a given mayoral administration cracked down on abusive construction it would face considerable work in documenting all the cases and prosecuting them. People fear, however, that there could be selective enforcement directed at particular families and this contributes to the political consensus for the Christian Democratic party, almost without its direct complicity. People also fear spiteful neighbors with whom they do not get along, because the latter may decide to file an anonymous charge at the town hall about abusive building. These must be investigated or the mayor faces being charged with the crime of omission of official acts. The penalty for abusive construction can result in municipal confiscation of the building, or even in its bulldozing and the exaction of a fine set at double the building's worth. When cases actually get prosecuted the penalties fall short of these dire outcomes because various legal cures, such as after-the-fact zoning variances, can be applied. But the potential troubles involved make people think twice about voting against the dominant party list at election time and influence their choices for preferential votes. There need not even be any direct threat from the party; their own complicity in the situation leads people to play it safe.

The social security system—old age and disability benefits and pensions, unemployment compensation, and medical insurance—is another area in which there is widely known and widespread application of real system strategies. On a regional level it is well documented that the Christian Democratic party, in consolidating its post-World War II position of power, developed a vast spoils system in the south that intertwined with this system (Clark, 1984: 348-373). Leftist parties level charges of "clientelism" at the DC for this. Those in power, even in Locorotondo, and some writers and scholars, rationalize the transfer of resources to people through such means by calling it a much needed subsidy that otherwise would not exist, to poor agricultural communities.

For example, certain kinds of disability entitle people either to disability pensions, which can be a helpful supplement to other income, or even to a job, often as a *bidello*, or hall porter/custodian, in a public institution of one kind or another. People in Locorotondo often talk about abuses of these rights. They say that disability pensions, for instance, can be obtained merely with the help of a doctor willing to sign the appropriate document. Patron-client relationships enter here, and create obligations at election time for those receiving such spoils. Certainly the halls of most public institutions, such as schools or government offices (all over Southern Italy, not just in Locorotondo) are overcrowded with hall porters who do very little.

In sum, the way people perceive things actually to operate implies for them two significant real system strategies. First, people perceive that to succeed in achieving what they need from bureaucracies they need to turn to patrons who can exert leverage for them, and personally see after their cases. Turning to such patrons for help creates obligations that lend them power. Second, they perceive that local custom can supersede law, especially if the latter places inconveniences upon them. There is a sense of birthright with respect to this—Locorotondo is a special place and all Locorotondesi ought to leave their fellow townspeople alone to invent their own real system strategies as long as no serious damage is done. However, those who control the enforcement of rules can gain power from the implicit threat that this lax approach might be retracted on an individual basis.

NOTES

1. The Italian Idiom used here is *"chi puo."* Literally this means "he who is able," and refers to someone with power or leverage in the local and perhaps more distant system of patron client relationships.

2. This is an example of "how *not* to ask an interview question." The question goes off in too many directions at once and is too long. Fortunately, the interviewee takes it in an interesting direction.

3. Kertzer (1980) describes a working-class Bolognese neighborhood, and how among Communists party institutions have in great part replaced church-oriented institutions.

4. See Barkan, 1986 for an excellent, although almost strictly Northern Italy focused, discussion of the history of the post-World War II Italian labor movement.

5. As I write, the Italian Communist Party has adopted a new name and set of symbols; it is now called the Party of the Democratic Left. The discrediting of Communist parties in Eastern Europe during 1989 and 1990 led to these changes.

6. Postmen helped people read and write letters, and even delivered love letters between courting young people informally without a stamp.

7. The importance of exchange in Southern European societies has long been remarked, and has been written about fairly extensively. At the basis of much of this writing was Foster's notion about dyadic contracts (1961).

8. Perhaps the earliest significant writings about social cohesion produced by lagged exchange are to be found in Marcel Mauss' essay "The Gift" (1966).

8 / Locorotondo in Southern Italian Perspective

Each Italian town is a place in itself, with singular pride, and difference of custom and character from other, even neighboring, towns. Yet each is also part of its region and part of the nation. I want to conclude this book by taking a brief look at Locorotondo in broader perspective within its region, and within Southern Italy as a whole, to underline how it participates in the broader culture and how it is unique.[1] I will adopt two approaches to this question. The first will be to explore both how local people view themselves as differentiated from other populations, and how they see themselves as akin to others in the broader region of Apulia and within Southern Italy. The latter will embrace a short examination of the stereotyping Southern Italians sometimes subject themselves to. The second will examine briefly a few socio-economic measures that show strong variations with respect to other places in Apulia and the South, and discuss their implications. The major implication is that people in Locorotondo have had it a little better than some of their Southern Italian compatriots.

HOW THE LOCOROTONDESI DISTINGUISH THEMSELVES FROM OTHER PEOPLES

The Locorotondesi see themselves as separate and unique in their area and in all of Southern Italy, although they also recognize kinship with other nearby towns and with Southerners from other parts of the *mezzogiorno*. What people choose to emphasize about their ethnic and regional identities at a given moment depends upon whether they are talking to compatriots or strangers, and how comfortable they are in the conversation. It also may depend upon shifting degrees of general frustration with society, or upon mood and personality. Many individuals talk as though they are proud of being Locorotondese and Southern Italian, others disparage the general qualities of Southern Italians, but accept and celebrate their identity as Locorotondesi. Others are soured upon both identities, but there are few of these. Most talk in lofty terms of their town.

Italians have a label for pride about one's home town: *campanilismo* or "bell-towerism." Most Locorotondesi are as *campanilistic* as other Italians, and enjoy celebrating the identity of their town and extolling its beauty and superiority over others. Such home town chauvinism unites Locorotondese people belonging to the subgroups that live there in a common focus with respect to other places, although each subgroup makes different choices about what to emphasize about the town. *Campanilismo* also lives on in the hearts of men and woman who have left Locorotondo for North Italy, or even abroad. It gets renewed when many emigrants return during the annual Festival of San Rocco held during the mid-August vacation period. Expressions of local pride include repeating folk beliefs and proverbs about other towns, kidding the dialects spoken in them, and celebrating Locorotondese identity by participating in customs, eating foods, and venerating saints associated with the town. There is even a slick magazine called, appropriately, *Locorotondo*, devoted to local things. (The reader will have noted that I have included passages from *Locorotondo* in previous chapters.)

In Southern Italy language itself carries messages about a person's origins. People mark local social boundaries the moment they speak, and doing so, they declare part of their identities. Language heard in everyday life falls into one of three categories: standard Italian, regional Italian, and local dialect. People speak the first two on formal occasions and with outsiders. For most people, including highly-educated ones, speaking truly standard Italian (based on the dialect of Florence, far to the North) involves a conscious effort. Teachers in the classroom make that effort, as do some politicians making speeches (although the clever local politician knows when to drop his discourse into dialectal speech to emphasize his ties with his constituency). For the elderly of the working classes standard Italian is often impossible. Southern Italian regional speech is intelligible with standard Italian. It involves an identifiable accent analogous to the regional accent found in parts of the United States such as the Southeast, and some minor vocabulary differences with standard Italian. In standard Italian, for instance, the word "now" is *ora*, or *adesso;* Southerners speaking acceptable regional Italian will say *mo*. Regional speech in Italian also can be tinged with habits carried over from dialect, depending very much on the educational attainment of the speaker. For instance, since in Locorotondo's dialect most words end in a consonant or in a weak and nondescript vowel, the less educated speaking Italian are often unsure about whether to end their nouns in the feminine "a," or the masculine "o." Their mistakes become immediate markers of their working class status in society.

However, most adults, most of the time, speak local dialect. Dialects are usually unintelligible with standard or regional Italian. People from neighboring towns readily understand one another's dialect, but also instantly recognize the differences. The dialects share most words, but between neighboring populations vowels differ slightly, or are put together in different combinations to make distinctive diphthongs. For instance, the Locorotondesi say *patreune* to mean "owner," or "boss," and the Fasanesi say *Patraume*.[2] Linguists recognize kinship between dialects of specific locals and have described families of dialects. Locorotondo's dialect belongs to the central Apulian group.

Even within Locorotondo's boundaries people distinguish minor dialect differences, especially between rural speech and town speech. This difference hinges mostly upon a small variation in the way people pronounce the *schwa* vowel (as in the "e" in "oven") when it falls between consonants. Although difficult for outsiders to notice or describe, town and country dwellers hear one another's speech as having a drawl. Also, toward the municipal borders rural dialects shade off toward the speech of the neighboring towns. This is particularly strong in the direction of Fasano for specific historical reasons. During the early nineteenth century many Fasanese families took land in perpetual lease in that zone.

Moving farther away, however, distinctions shade off into dialect family differences that make mutual intelligibility difficult. People from Locorotondo have some trouble understanding the northern Apulian dialects. There would be special difficulties farther down the Italian heel toward the city of Lecce, where the dialects are more like Calabrian and Sicilian speech. Finally, someone speaking a Central or Northern Italian dialect, say Roman, or Venetian, would confront high barriers to communication. Confronted with people who would speak another dialect in everyday speech, individuals who can muster something closer to standard Italian do so, and consider it discourteous to use dialect with strangers. Nowadays only a few elderly people can speak no Italian at all.

Dialect barriers typical of the Italian Peninsula have gradually worn away during the twentieth century. At first, this occurred with the extension of schooling to more people. Later, it continued with the wide diffusion of radio and television, which have brought standard Italian speech into the homes of many families where it was never heard before. It is now common to travel in North Italy and hear regionally accented Italian, not dialect, spoken in everyday street conversation. Although this is not yet true in the South, especially in rural areas, as noted in Chapter 4, things were changing by the early 1980s when I did the initial fieldwork for this study. Locorotondese parents, including rural parents, made an effort to speak to their children in Italian because they felt that they would do better in school if they arrived in the classroom speaking the national language instead of needing to be taught it as a second language. Therefore, in another generation the rich dialectal speech now used by adults in Locorotondo may be a relic. This either means that people will give other expressions of local identity more emphasis, or that they will begin to see themselves as belonging to larger social entities than previously defined by dialects.

There are other dialect-like differences in areas of culture besides language, and some of these are likely to remain strong in the future. In the past such differences were very strong. For instance, each town had its own ideas about how to measure things, and a complete set of local weights and measures to do so. To illustrate, in Locorotondo the traditional land measure—the *tomolo*—contained eight *stoppelli*, but in Fasano a *tomolo* contained seven. For vineyards, there was a special measure, the *quartiero*, which approximately equaled a *stoppello*. Moving farther away, completely different measurement names and quantities cropped up. The centralized imposition of the metric system for legal measurement eroded this, but senior members of society still informally talk about many different amounts in local measures.

Foods also vary among towns, although just as there is a cluster of related dialects, there is a regional cuisine. Locorotondo prides itself on its *ngiummeridde*, tripe rolled up around a stuffing and stewed in broth. There was once even a festival organized around this food by the local "cultural developers," two women employed by the municipality to oversee the town's cultural life. Another particularly local dish is *tridde*, a soup made with tiny dumplings pinched from a ball of stiff dough. Of course, few Locorotondese meals would be without *Bianco di Locorotondo*, the town's renowned white wine. This is perhaps the truly special thing a Locorotondese host can offer. Connoisseurs know Apulian cuisine for roasted meats (this reflects the area's historical dependence upon pastoralism), and the peculiar form of pasta known as *orecchietti*, or "little ears," made by drawing a table knife over a small lump of dough to produce an ear shape. Mothers serve this with tomato sauce, but also with a local form of broccoli (*cima di rape*) and anchovies. Locorotondese women often make *orecchietti* from whole wheat flour. Sometimes the knives which women utilized to make *orecchietti* in the past become sentimental keepsakes for their daughters. Most people eat them as first course in a Sunday meal. Even fruits and vegetables have local forms. Typical of the Locorotondo/ Fasano zone is the *barattiere*, a delicious round cucumber that is almost as sweet as a melon. Of course, foods also vary according to their availability in various zones, and before refrigeration and truck transport people ate only local products. A proverb turns symbolically upon this inexperience with things produced in neighboring areas: "In Fasano wine turned to vinegar; in Locorotondo, rotten fish; in Martina Franca, bitter olive oil." The Fasano coastline produces fish and olive oil; Locorotondo and Martina Franca produce wine.

Campanilistic lore includes proverbs that celebrate the glories of Locorotondo, such as the adolescent saying (heard proudly from a Locorotondese teenage girl): "Girls from Locorotondo have nice round behinds." (It loses its rhyme in translation: *I pecciuèdde de Curdunne onne i cule tunne tunne*.) It also includes slurs on both neighboring Martina Franca and Fasano such as the proverb: "The Martinese [peasant] sows lead shot [instead of seed]." People from Locorotondo stereotype those from Fasano as less than honest and those from Martina Franca as stubborn. The Fasano stereotype has a basis in truth, unfortunately. In the early 1980s the town had become a well-known crossroads for Southern Italian drug traffic and its streets were not safe at night. The Locorotondese saying goes that the Martinesi "have half an hour," which means that they have half an hour a day when they reason according to their own incomprehensible logic. In turn, those towns have their own stereotypes and sayings about Locorotondo. For instance, to underline their opinion that the Locorotondesi are naive and do not get around much, the Fasanese proverb says: "Said the one from Locorotondo [upon visiting the coast]: the sea, the sea, and that is all made of water!"

Each Southern Italian town differs from others in matters of belief. The most prominent thing in this realm is the identity of the saints venerated in a town. In Locorotondo, San Rocco, and San Giorgio are the two pre-eminent saints. The association of the warrior Saint George with Locorotondo goes back into the early middle ages when the settlement on the ridge was probably named Casale San Giorgio. San Rocco became the town's protector when the population was spared an epidemic raging through the region during 1690-1691 (Baccaro, 1968: 33). The frequency of men named Rocco and Giorgio is high in Locorotondo. As I noted earlier, people celebrate San Rocco in August with a grandiose *festa* that draws the town's diaspora home. This celebrates the Locorotondesi as a people. On the other hand, the town commemorates San Giorgio for two days in April with processions both inside and outside the church that emphasize the symbolism of civic authority.

The mayor plays a special part, decked out in his official shoulder to waist tricolored sash, and the municipal police march in uniform, followed by veterans' organizations and other official groups. The Roman Catholic Church denied Saint George his sainthood several decades ago. The occasion of his day is therefore quite local, and I noted that during the sermon given at a Mass held as part of the festivities, the priest said little about Saint George's sainthood, although he portrayed the ex-saint as an ideal of courage. Martina Franca's patron is Saint Martin, Alberobello's are the twin healer Saints Cosmo and Damian, and Fasano's is Saint John the Baptist. Each has a major feast and people from Locorotondo and other neighboring towns often attend, nowadays for fun and for religious reasons. In the past, because saints' festivals corresponded with livestock fairs, they were also important in local commerce.

Figure 8.1   A stopping point in the procession for Saint George. Bearers for the heavy statue are being changed.

There are differences in folk beliefs between towns as well. For instance, I noted before that many people in Locorotondo's countryside believe in the *ajure* who comes in the night and sits on a person's chest paralyzing movement and leaving bruises and tangled hair in the morning. Local folk belief also admits the existence of an elf-like creature called the *monachidde*, "little monk," who helps by doing chores in the stalls. Other nearby populations in the Province of Bari also recognize various little people, but give them different labels and ascribe different combinations of characteristics to them. For instance, the "little monk" name, in one variant or another, often labels a nasty being more like the *ajure*, not a helpful one. Some Apulian populations recognize a household spirit called the "Patron of the household" who must be asked permission before crossing the threshold of a new house (Sada, 1978). As with the vowels in local dialects, similar elements appear in different combinations and permutations from town to town within the region. Culture, like language, shows considerable dialectal variation.

Then there is Locorotondo's roundness. Recall that the name of the town means "round place." Although it is oval, the old town, which was originally circled by a wall with towers, has a round feeling to it. This is especially because of the *lungomare*, a road and sidewalk with a railing, that descends around the town's southern side following the old curve once occupied by the wall. (People say "*lungomare*," or "shore road," because there is a fine, long view from it, and because it reminds them of similar roads and walks in nearby coastal cities.) No neighboring towns have the compact circularity of Locorotondo's historical center. Even the public garden has a circular path around it. Teens remark that in Martina Franca young people promenade back and forth in the public gardens, but in Locorotondo they circle the park. This may seem a small distinction, but local people see it as crucial because life in the public gardens is significant. In fact, a local essayist has celebrated roundness as an emblem of "Locorotondoness" in a piece in the town's magazine. He not only referred to the physical circularity of the town and its public garden, but extended it into a metaphor to describe what he thought was a self-contained quality and perhaps a closedness typical of the Locorotondese world view (Calella, 1987). Doing so, he contributed to Locorotondo's conversation about itself—its own continual definition and redefinition of identity. Here the conversation, which otherwise might have occurred while musing over things with friends, became "pickled" for posterity. (Consider also Tété and Tutuccio's discussion of the town's roundness in Chapter 5.)

Locorotondo's country folk are quick to point out that, although the Murgia dei Trulli forms an area typified by peasant settlement in the countryside, the settlement pattern of their town is the most extreme case. They note, for instance, that in Martina Franca peasants lived in town and moved out to trulli only during peaks work times of the year. They also note that historically in Martina, as in other nearby towns, there was a labor market in a main square where farm hands would muster at sunrise hoping to be hired for a day's work. No one remembers a time when this was true in Locorotondo because the entirety of the peasantry lived in the countryside, and landowners contracted for agricultural laborers individually. This is a point of pride for country people because it underlines their value of self-sufficiency.

Another strong point of campanilistic pride among the country residents is their attitude about work. In Locorotondo work is not only a matter of livelihood. It has become a symbol around which a whole population rallies to assert and celebrate its general superiority over other populations. In conversations about the success of Locorotondese construction workers and contractors, rural people contrast this with inferior attitudes they believe to be held elsewhere. They hold that Locorotondese workers receive preference all over the region because of the solid day's work they put in for their pay. Even town dwellers, who cannot participate directly in the self-adulatory attitudes of their rural cousins, vicariously hail their town by pointing to the general prosperity of "their" peasants and the resulting beauty of "their" countryside. They can point also to the labor of the artisan class from before, but have to admit that the attitudes about work and technical virtuosity that epitomized that segment of society are dying with the last practitioners, and the end of hand labor.

Another largely middle-class celebration of "Locorotondoness" has come about during several historical periods with the loving publication of cultural and historical magazines and a few local scholarly works. A major institution in Locorotondo, the local cooperatively founded savings bank, has financed recent publications through its profits. Others have found their way into print with help from the municipality. Locorotondo is not unusual for having a devoted group of local intellectuals, most of them teachers at one level or another, who write and publish sporadic magazines and pamphlets and even books about local things. Many small towns have such groups, and they preserve a valuable cultural heritage. However, these writings are not merely compilations of interesting historical, folkloric, biographical, literary, and even natural historical texts. Their very existence makes important statements about how middle-class people, for whom writing and scholarship, especially of an historical nature, have symbolic power, come together around the home town as an idea that is important enough to have a series of writings devoted to it. I am sure that some among the local intellectual community would argue with some things I have published in Italian in the local magazine *Locorotondo*, in other articles in English (a language which some of them can read), or in this and my other book. However, I am also sure that even they take pleasure in the idea that someone has come from far-off Wisconsin to take part in the conversation about their town. What I have said now exists alongside the texts they have produced. My words should not be seen as written with a more authoritative voice than theirs, especially because I have written with totally different goals in mind. Taken all together these texts about Locorotondo help portray some of its reality for those who will come along in the future and themselves join in the conversation.

The symbolic value of these publications has greatest meaning for the new middle class. Little that is of particular significance to the country-dwelling population sees print despite their large contribution to the population. This is not so much an elite class bias, as it derives from the historical experience of the current town middle class, which is mostly composed of children and grandchildren of the artisan working class. Reminiscences about craftsmen abound in *Locorotondo* magazine. There is another magazine, published in Martina Franca, that fills an elite symbolic niche. It celebrates the plateau zone as a whole, growing nostalgic about the days of big landowners and their large estates.

HOW LOCOROTONDESI TALK ABOUT THEMSELVES
WITHIN THEIR REGION

I have explored some ways people from Locorotondo like to distinguish themselves from other populations in South Italy. In other words, I have explored some of their perceptions about what it means to be Locorotondese. I must now address another related question. This concerns how the Locorotondesi see themselves as belonging to the general Apulian and Southern Italian population. Such perceptions, as one might guess, are likely to reflect matters and institutions that transcend the boundaries of the town and its hinterlands.

Before the changes that culminated in modern Locorotondo—until well into the 1950s—most Locorotondese people lived their daily lives and conducted their affairs well within the boundaries of the municipality. The exceptions were the landowning and professional elites, who tended to have networks of friends and relatives that extended farther, the more ambitious craftsmen who sold their wares at markets in other towns, and some rural people who had occasion to go to saints' festivals in other towns to worship or buy and sell livestock at the associated fairs. Also, two world wars and compulsory military service pulled young men away from their families and gave them a taste of other places to which, for the most part, women had no access. Once the war was over, or military service completed, however, most men returned to spend the rest of their lives close to home. Early in the century a few others experienced emigration, but often in a Southern Italian enclave that strongly insulated them from the host culture and language.

The arrival and diffusion of automobiles and public transportation have broadened the horizons of most Locorotondesi beyond their town. Many people now conduct a part of their weekly affairs in towns and cities other than Locorotondo. A particularly strong factor in this has been travel to nearby towns to continue education beyond middle school. Further, the quest for employment based upon that education has also forced many to find jobs in nearby towns. This has especially been true of teachers and others who are public employees. Many have work friends with whom they socialize in other towns because of this. As I noted in an earlier chapter, many men from both town and country work in heavy industry at the Italsider steel mill in Taranto. Rural contractors and construction workers commute to other towns daily. Also, certain family business matters, such as dealing with the electric utility, mean a trip to a nearby town.

For many families the summer brings days, or even weeks, in nearby Adriatic beach resorts. This would have been very difficult for any but the most wealthy until the diffusion of cars in the 1960s. A trip to either the Gulf of Taranto coast or the Adriatic shore means stopping at a market to get fresh shellfish to bring home to the plateau for a special meal. Many Locorotondesi have become connoisseurs of the mussels and tiny nut-flavored clams (true *vongole*) that come from Taranto. People from Locorotondo go to other towns in the area to enjoy patron saint festivals or historical pageants. Religious people also go on bus excursions to sites in the area where they believe there have been apparitions of the Virgin Mary, or even on overnight trips to the Vatican in Rome. People also travel far more widely to shop for household items and clothing than they did in the decades following World War

II. There are department stores and supermarkets in both Fasano and Martina Franca, and some people make trips to Bari or Taranto to make their purchases. Local hunters make pilgrimages all the way to the wooded mountain sides of Basilicata, and fishermen descend to the coasts. For those with historical interests, the wealth of attractions ranges from the Roman excavations at nearby Egnazia to the fine medieval churches found in many Apulian cities. The insularity that characterized the Locorotondese world view, before travel was a possibility for very many people, has given way to an attitude that values the town and its way of life very highly, but within the context of an appreciation for a broader variety of things Apulian.

On the other hand, part of the way many Locorotondesi see themselves reflects a general Southern Italian love/hate relationship with being Southern Italian. This involves an ambivalent self-stereotype developed from images of Southern Italians and their culture held in the North, and from the economic marginality of the South. In upper Italy many people continue to think of Southerners, almost in racial terms, as inferior. Common Northern images about Southern Italians contain a litany of negativities including laziness, lack of organization, primitiveness, stupidity, craftiness, violence, dishonesty, and male jealousy and hypersexuality, among others. Southerners who go north to work in factories, or for other reasons, such as attending a Northern university, must put up with such attitudes about their "mentality," and sometimes with being called names like *terrone*, "person of the dirt." It is inescapable that most of Italy's industrialization, and the wealth and modernity associated with it, exists in North and Central Italy, and that much of the South still suffers from economic marginality, some of it extreme. Northerners often blame this on the Southerners themselves and their "mentality," without considering the complex historical reasons for disparities between the regions of Italy. Then, also, the South hosts pockets of criminality—*mafia* in Western Sicily, *camorra* in Naples, *'ndrangete* in parts of Calabria. These make sensational headlines that people too easily blame on Southern ethnicity, again without considering the complexities of historical experience and socio-economic conditions from which they arose.[3] Northerners often assign negative stereotypes to Southerners, but the latter often swallow them too, coming to accept, at least for some purposes, the views of the politically and economically dominant North.[4]

For instance, an exasperating commonplace I have heard both in Locorotondo and in other places in the South is that the allied forces should have remained in occupation after the World War II so that the place would have some organization. (Sometimes people invoke the Germans instead of the allies, and very few wistfully recall the "order" that Mussolini's Fascism brought.) This comes out of frustrations with the inefficiencies of government. A Locorotondese businessman I interviewed about the problems with entrepreneurial activity in the South, lamented the lack of risk-taking behavior, highlighting a concern among Southern Italians about wanting an immediate pay-off to activities. He felt that long-term planning and building of businesses represented a leap that stopped both local would-be entrepreneurs and local financial institutions psychologically. He called this attitude "laziness" (*pigrizia*), but then continued that he did not view laziness in a totally negative sense. Perhaps, he said, it was better that local people would rather go out to the country to enjoy the cherry blossoms than become too attached to the entrepreneurial spirit.

Part of what many Locorotondesi think about themselves as Southern Italians is a mirror image of the North Italian stereotype about them. Perhaps, the stereotype says, they do not organize things very well, and perhaps they are blocked from business risk taking by their culture and historical experience, but they are also friendly, casual, family oriented, and enjoy life. Different aspects of the stereotype can be used for different conversational purposes and to express a variety of moods.

Another part of the fitful lament many Locorotondesi sing about Southern Italian culture has to do with the workings of the official and real systems, as I laid them out in the last chapter. On one hand there is a certain respect for the clever manipulator of the those systems—for the person who can use bureaucracy to the advantage of friends and relatives. From another perspective, people from Locorotondo describe the very existence of the patron-client system as a corruption of the more democratic way things ought to work, and ascribe it to a stereotypical view of Southern Italian character, which many characterize as too greedy and self-interested. Sometimes people broaden these ideas beyond the regional stereotype to encompass being Italian in general. This is especially true when some national scandal involving the public interest explodes in the media, as is often the case in Italy.

SOME OBSERVATIONS ON HOW LOCOROTONDO MAY BE DISTINGUISHED FROM OTHER PLACES

To deepen our understanding of Locorotondo in comparative perspective, I now turn to looking at just a few observations that highlight differences from a regional viewpoint. The views of its inhabitants aside, let me observe and measure some differences between Locorotondo and other Southern Italian places, and discuss their implications. Southern Italy has been the subject of a social scientific and historical literature to which Italian authors have contributed since the eighteenth century, and to which international observers have contributed mostly during the post-World War II era. That literature has always highlighted "the problems of the south," and descriptions of Southern underdevelopment, poverty, and misery are quite common. The South has been portrayed as if it were a Third World country by many writers.[5] Few have examined Southern situations like Locorotondo, where a somewhat higher degree of security and comfort have existed since the nineteenth century.

The troubles that have been faced by most Southern Italian rural people are many. They include poor housing, poor health conditions, chronic unemployment and underemployment, the oppression of being at the bottom of a rigid social class structure, and constant financial insecurity. Added to these are the natural disasters—earthquakes, volcanic eruptions, floods—that parts of the South suffer periodically, and the devastation of land through overuse and erosion. A keen observer of the economically marginal Southern Italian scene is Anne Cornelisen, who went there to help as a social worker, not as a scholar. Describing conditions in a town in Basilicata (she uses the older term Lucania) where she worked, she writes,

> Long into the night the alleys will echo with the fights and confusions of ten thousand people living piled one on top of the other in space too small for half the number. They

seek the warmth of human company as horses in a pasture huddle in a corner for protection against the wind. In the past this crowding meant protection against the unknown. Neighbors are not chosen; in most cases they resent and envy one another; but their physical closeness and the unwritten law of mutual assistance, however grudging, give protection against the caprices of a vengeful God. For the terrifying unknowns of the twentieth century in Lucania are those natural calamities which are endemic and more devastating than bubonic plague or armies of Saracens. A landslide carries off or buries an entire town. A great crevasse opens up to swallow a field during an earthquake. A roof suddenly gives way in the middle of the night, killing ten people. A child who was healthy yesterday is dying today of "evil spirits in the tummy." A strong young woman after a winter cold begins wasting away with tuberculosis (1969: 15)

The more typical settlement pattern for Apulia was one by which those who tilled the soil, usually farm workers, lived in town, often cheek by jowl with each other and the other local working classes in cramped, ill-ventilated, rented, quarters, usually at street level. Pitkin, in his evocative book *The House that Giacomo Built* (1985), describes such housing for Stilo in Calabria. There a one room house, partitioned inside to provide some degree of privacy, was typical, and the few women who stood to inherit such dwellings became highly desirable marriage partners (1985: 21). Among the worst cases in the South were the cave dwellings

Figure 8.2   Calvello, a small agritown in the mountains of Basilicata. Hometown of the author's maternal great grandfather.

inhabited by farm workers in the sides of the stark bluffs of Matera in Basilicata (see figure 1.1). (Ironically, now that they are no longer inhabited, these are a tourist attraction.) In Matera poverty and misery reigned (Tentori, 1976).[6] Although not confined to caves, the farm worker inhabitants of Northern Apulian towns in Foggia Province, and northern interior areas of Bari Province also lived under dreadful conditions (Snowden, 1986: 61). Even now, in such towns the traveler finds large working class neighborhoods composed of tiny squalid dwellings.[7]

Locorotondo is part of a larger region, comprising parts of the provinces of Bari, Brindisi, and Taranto, that an early twentieth century geographer labeled the *Murgia dei Trulli,* or "Plateau of the Trulli," based on the peculiar sort of rural construction I described earlier. The general area is also characterized by the presence of many people living in the countryside farming small holdings. Since small-holder intensive agriculture has been rare in a Southern Italy marked by landlessness, large populations of agricultural workers, and tenuous forms of land tenure such as sharecropping, the plateau where Locorotondo lies is unusual. Historically Locorotondo may have set the pattern of dispersed settlement for the area. It has always had the highest degree of this kind of settlement for the whole zone, as it does now. (see figure 8.3). Neighboring Cisternino is most like Locorotondo in this respect.

While rural settlement has been good for the peasant and postpeasant populations, having half the population living in the countryside has created political peculiarities in Locorotondo. It has created problems for politicians because of the

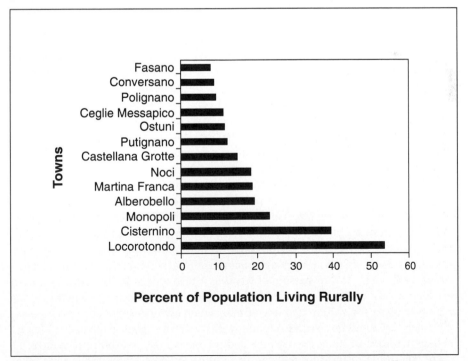

Figure 8.3   The distribution of the percent of population living rurally among the towns on the Plateau of the Trulli (data from Liuzzi, 1981: 150). See Figure 1.2 for locations.

greater difficulty of mobilizing and maintaining control over votes in the rural segment of the population. This problem was addressed in the post-World War II era when the Monarchist party (which no longer has any strength) established a network of "hamlet bosses" in the countryside. Such men served as a patron-client link between the *jazzeile* and the town political structure, and for a few years the Monarchist party captured the mayoralty based on rural votes. Threatened, the Christian Democratic party followed suit establishing its own network of "hamlet bosses," and managed to recapture most of the rural voters and incorporate them into its patron-client network.

Similarly, the rurally settled population in Locorotondo has created problems for public administrators that are not faced by many of their counterparts in agritown settings where few people live in the countryside. Such problems became clear as early as the 1820s. Recall from Chapter 2 that the town's elite tried to force the removal of the peasantry from the countryside in 1827, probably for problems of control and administration, among others. Recently, there has been a demand for services such as garbage collection, electrification, road paving, and aqueduct water from the rural population as it has moved away from its peasant identity into being a bedroom community for contractors and skilled construction artisans, as well as a collection of part-time agriculturalists. Country families wish to enjoy the open spaces of the countryside while simultaneously enjoying the amenities of a more urban lifestyle. Mayors and assessors face the expense of providing services to a population of around 5,000 people who live scattered over a territory as large as a city. Part of the recent political capital captured by the Christian Democratic party rests on its ability to activate patron client networks at higher levels and find funding to extend modern services to the rural population gradually. By the early 1980s, for instance, nearly all rural roads in Locorotondo were paved, and nearly all rural areas had electricity. Other services were coming.

Locorotondo's settlement pattern also corresponds to high levels of home ownership for the area. About 82 percent of Locorotondese families either own their dwellings, or enjoy some other rent-free title to them. Most rental property is in the town center, and there an available apartment or house is very difficult to find.[8] It is mostly transient outsiders, like policemen or anthropologists, who need to rent housing. In Bari Province, to which Locorotondo belongs, among 48 municipalities, the aggregate figure for ownership or other rent-free title is about 62 percent, and the range is between about 50 percent and 84 percent.[9] In Locorotondo, this high level of home ownership, especially given the relative comfort of much of the housing in question, further reflects the relatively higher level of security typical of the town and its hinterlands. Locorotondo's country-dwelling peasants, who have provided their children with housing at marriage for generations, greatly sustain this pattern. Although, now ownership of housing is also typical in the town, as Ciccio the tailor noted in his interview, it was not just a few decades ago when life was more precarious for artisans and few of them could own housing. The development of the new town middle class has brought with it improvements in quality of life that include the hope of home ownership, and for many, the possibility to realize it.

Another kind of measure that can be used to compare Locorotondo with other Apulian and Southern places has to do with the concentration or diffusion of wealth.

Until very recently, in Southern Italy the primary measure of wealth has been land ownership. All too often land has been concentrated in few hands, impoverishing the majority. A good statistic to use for describing uniformity or concentration in the distribution of wealth is called the Gini coefficient (G). This number is easy to understand because as it approaches 1.0 there is greater concentration into fewer hands, and when it approaches 0, each owner has the same amount as every other owner. Graphing the Gini coefficients that describe concentration of land for the same *Murgia dei Trulli* towns shown in Figure 8.1. shows that Locorotondo and Cisternino again come close to each other in having the most uniform distributions of land.

There is also a relationship between farm size and concentration of land. Generally, among the towns in question, as the farm size decreases so will the Gini coefficient. Therefore Locorotondo and its neighbors stand at one end of a range in these matters, and represent a type of town in which most peasant families have lived in the countryside on small amounts of land that is more uniformly distributed among households than in most other towns in the zone. Such differences were even more pronounced in the past, because during the late 1940s and early 1950s there were land reform programs in Southern Italy that broke up some great estates and redistributed land. Therefore Gini coefficients in the immediate post-World War II years were higher for many Apulian towns than they are now. Since this was not

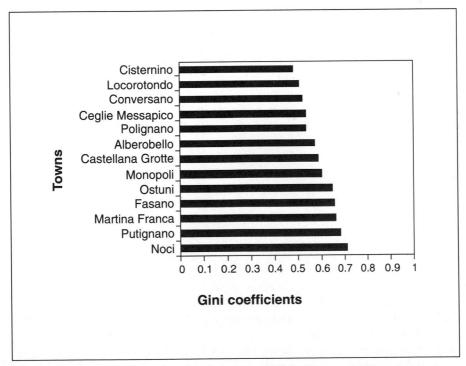

Figure 8.4   The distribution of Gini coefficients for land ownership among the towns on the Plateau of the Trulli. As the Gini coefficient decreases, land is more uniformly distributed. (Data elaborated from ISTAT, 1972: Fasc. 74–76, Table 18.)

true in Locorotondo, where land was already uniformly distributed and the pattern of small proprietorship well developed, the difference in Gini coefficient was more extreme. Ranging farther from the *Murgia dei Trulli*, and including all the towns in the three provinces (Bari, Brindisi, and Taranto) in which it lies, there are much higher concentrations of land in some areas, although again current statistics do not reflect this in the way they would have before land reforms.

The wide distribution of land in Locorotondo coupled with its intensive cultivation with grapes as a cash crop, has meant a degree of security for its rural population, compared to the largely landless, or land poor, farm worker populations of many Southern Italian towns. Locorotondo's was not a wealthy peasantry by any means. However, the historical adaptive strategy of Locorotondo's peasants allowed them greater comfort than dreamed of by rural people in many other areas of the South. The adaptive strategy of Locorotondese peasants, the reader will recall, was based upon the development of vineyards through perpetual lease contracts, and there resulted a high degree of peasant self-sufficiency based upon hard work and frugality. The observation made by town and country people alike, that an early morning, town square labor market never existed in Locorotondo testifies to peasant self-sufficiency. Those who wanted to employ workers had to seek them out. These things have been part of Locorotondo's historical experience, and even though land is not the sole basis of wealth any longer, the attitudes that arose before color the way people now think about wealth and status.

To some extent people from Locorotondo have known aspects of poverty more typical of the rest of the South—especially those old enough to remember the lean years of the depression, or the disruption of life caused by World War II. Until the post-war years medical care was expensive and not readily available. They still lack facilities, and diseases that would be routinely treatable in the United States or Northern Europe still take lives in rural Locorotondo. The artisan's and peasant's life of hard work took its tolls. Hoeing bent the spine; working in a small damp workshop in town, or breathing limestone dust, could lead to respiratory problems. There were times of crisis, and there were times when there was less to eat than people hoped for. For the rural population of Locorotondo, however, such times were exceptional. Constant poverty and misery were not the expectation of a lifetime, as they were for the agricultural populations of towns such as the one Anne Cornelisen described. Most people who have grown up in the countryside could expect to inherit some land and have a house built for them upon marriage. They could expect to have enough to eat if they worked very hard and lived frugally. They could expect to provide for their children, and before social welfare systems came along, they could expect that their children would provide for them when they grew old. If they emigrated it was usually to build a better life for themselves back home in Locorotondo. Those who grew up in town had it worse to begin with, and suffered deeply from the crisis in artisan production that occurred in the 1960s. But even there, emigration and return often brought about a new way of life through savings or new training, and the explosion in education, retail selling, and needs for repair services provided new jobs. To a certain extent these improvements have occurred all over Southern Italy, but Locorotondo, for peculiar historical reasons concerning its secure and productive country dwelling peasantry, already had a leg up. One who visits and walks the streets of the historical center, the expanding periphery, and the roads of the countryside, must think that, whatever the conditions of the past, whatever the crises met by the town's citizens through the years, Locorotondo is now a fine place to live.

NOTES

1. This is an old theme in the study of peasant cultures. Kroeber, for instance, defined peasant societies as constituting "part-societies with part-cultures" (1948: 284). By this he meant that each peasant village was different from each other one and from the overall society to which it belonged in some ways, but that each also reflected and participated in the greater society.

2. See Figure 1.2 to locate the other towns mentioned in these passages.

3. There is little writing about *camorra* or *'ndrangete* in English, but the reader interested in *mafia* in Sicily will benefit from Schneider and Schneider, 1976; and Blok, 1974, which develop specific historical understandings for the rise of *mafia* activity that move away from simply blaming them on Sicilian "mentality," or "world view." Both interpretations, and many historical analyses of the origins of Southern lagging development, point to an almost colonial relationship with the economically dominant North as significant in shaping the contemporary South.

4. Although difficult for the non-specialist reader, Herzfeld (1987) exhaustively examines similar ideas of nationalism and self-view for Greece.

5. Some key writings on aspects of Southern Italian underdevelopment that are accessible in English include: Belmonte, 1979; Cornelisen 1969, 1976; Dolci, 1959; Lopreato, 1967; and Snowden, 1986.

6. A vivid sense of this for Matera, and for a nearby town, can be gained from Carlo Levi's semi-autobiographical novel *Christ Stopped at Eboli* (1947), which is about his political confinement in an isolated Southern town during the fascist era.

7. Farther away, but not untypical of what many Southern Italians have faced, are the agritowns of Sicily. Housing conditions in the post-World War II decades in rural Sicily were dreadful as Dolci describes them in his book *Waste* (1964).

8. There is more and more development of rural property for summer rental to tourists, but this does not reflect year-round housing patterns.

9. The data are reported in Table 16, Volume 2, Number 72 (Bari) of ISTAT, 1983.

References

Allen, Edward
    1969 *Stone Shelters*. Cambridge, Mass.: M.I.T. Press.

Ancona, Sante
    1988 La Lunga Notte di Teté e Tutuccio. *Locorotondo* 3: 113-127.

Arlacchi, Pino
    1980 *Mafia, Contadini, e Latifondo nella Calabria Tradizionale*. Bologna, Il Mulino.

Baccaro, Giuseppe
    1968 *Memorie Storiche di Locorotondo*. Locorotondo: Biblioteca del Lavoratore.

Banfield, Edward C.
    1958 *The Moral Basis of a Backward Society*. Glencoe: The Free Press.

Barkan, Joanne
    1986 *Visions of Emancipation*. New York: Praeger.

Belmonte, Thomas
    1979 *The Broken Fountain*. New York, Columbia University Press.

Bennett, John Bennett
    1969 *The Northern Plainsmen: Adaptive Strategy and Agrarian Life*. Chicago: Aldine.

Blok, Anton
    1974 *The Mafia of a Sicilian Village, 1860 to 1960*. Oxford: Blackwells.

Brandes, Stanley
    1980 *Metaphors of Masculinity: Sex and Status in Andalusian Folklore*. Philadelphia: University of Pennsyvania Press.

Calella, Giampiero
    1987 Contributi per una Definizione della Psicologia Locorotondese. *Locorotondo* 2: 75-77.

Calella, Sigismondo
    1941 *Colonizzazione e Ruralizzazione. Un Modello: Il Territorio di Locorotondo*. Martina Franca, Aquaro e Dragonetti.

Church, E. M.
    1895 *Chapters in an Adventurous Life: Sir Richard Church in Italy and Greece*. Edinburgh and London: W. Blackwood and Sons.

Clark, Martin
    1984 *Modern Italy 1972-1982*. London and New York: Longman.

Cofano, Antonio
    1977 *Storia antifeudale della Franca Martina*. Fasano: Schena Editore.

Consoli, N.
    1988 Francesco Consoli: Un Profilo. *Locorotondo* 3: 137-150.

Cornelisen, Anne
1969 *Torregreca*. London: Macmillan.

———
1976 *Women of the Shadows*. New York: Random House.
Dolci, Danilo
1959 *Report from Palermo*. New York: Viking Press.

———
1964 *Waste: An Eyewitness Report on Some Aspects of Waste in Western Sicily*. New York
    Monthly Review Press.
Foster, George
1961 The Dyadic Contract: A Model for the Social Structure of a Mexican Village.
    American Anthropologist 63: 1173-92.
Galt, Anthony H.
1974 Rethinking Patron Client Relationships: the Real System and the Official System in
    Southern Italy. *Anthropological Quarterly* 47: 182-202.

———
1991a *Far from the Church Bells: Settlement and Society in an Apulian Town*. Cambridge,
    U.K.: Cambridge University Press.

———
1991b Magical Harm in Locorotondo. *American Ethnologist* 18: 735–750.
Guarella, Giuseppe
1983 *La chiesa della Greca in Locorotondo*. Locorotondo: Cassa Rurale e Artigiana.
Herzfeld, Michael
1987 *Anthropology Through the Looking Glass*. Cambridge, U. K.: Cambridge University
    Press.
Hufford, David J.
1982 *The Terror that Comes in the Night*. Philadephia: University of Pennsylvania Press.
ISTAT (Istituto Centrale di Statistica)
1933 *Catasto Agrario 1929* vol. *VIII*. Compartimento delle Puglie. Provincia di Bari.
    Fascicolo 71. Rome: Instituto Poligrafico dello Stato.

———
1972 *Secondo Censimento Generale dell'Agricoltura*. Rome, Istituto Centrale di Statis-
    tica.

———
1983 *Dodicesimo Censimento Generale della Popolazione*, 25 Ottobre 1981. Roma:
    Istituto Centrale di Statistica.
Kertzer, David
1980 *Comrades and Christians: Religion and Political Struggle in Communist Italy*.
    Cambridge, U. K.: Cambridge University Press.
Kroeber, Alfred L.
1948 *Anthropology*. New York: Harcourt Brace and Company.
Levi, Carlo
1947 *Christ Stopped at Eboli: the Story of a Year*. New York: Farrar, Strauss and
    Company.
Lisi, Arcangelo
n.d. *Storia del Movimento Operaio di Locorotondo*. Locorotondo: Arti Grafiche Angelini
    e Pace.

Liuzzi, Achille
    1981 *La Murgia dei Trulli: Lineamenti Caratteristiche, Sviluppo Economico e Civile.*
        Martina Franca: Nettuno.

Lopreato, Joseph
    1967 *Peasants No More.* San Francisco: Chandler Publishing Company.

Mauss, Marcel
    1966 *The Gift.* London: Cohen and West.

Mills, C. Wright
    1959 *The Sociological Imagination.* New York: Grove Press, Inc.

Palasciano, Italo
    1986 Locorotondo: viticoltura anni trenta; primi anni di vita della Cantina Sociale.
        Umanesimo della Pietra, numero unico (July '86): 29–40.

———
    1987 Trasformazioni agrarie e nascita dell'industria vinicola. *Umanesimo e la Pietra*, July
        1987: 93–101.

Pitkin, Donald S.
    1985 *The House That Giacomo Built.* Cambridge: Cambridge University Press.

Ricchioni, Vincenzo
    1958 Miracoli del lavoro contadino; i vigneti della Murgia dei "Trulli". *Annali della
        Facoltá di Agraria dell'Universitá di Bari* 14: 347-381.

Sada, Luigi
    1978 Un Singolare Rituale Barese. *Societá di Storia Patria per la Puglia. Studi e Ricerche.*
        1: 261-279.

Sampietro, Giuseppe
    1922 *Fasano: Indagini Storiche* (rielaborazione di Angelo Custodero). Fasano: Schena
        editore.

Schneider, Jane and Peter Schneider
    1976 *Culture and Political Economy in Western Sicily.* New York: Academic Press.

Snowden, Frank M.
    1986 *Violence and Great Estates in the South of Italy: Apulia, 1900-1922.* Cambridge,
        U. K.: Cambridge University Press.

Tentori, Tullio
    1976 Social classes and family in a Southern Italian town: Matera. In John G. Peristiany,
        ed., *Mediterranean Family Structures.* Cambridge, U. K.: Cambridge University
        Press.